SpringerBriefs in Psychology

SpringerBriefs present concise summaries of cutting-edge research and practical applications across a wide spectrum of fields. Featuring compact volumes of 55 to 125 pages, the series covers a range of content from professional to academic. Typical topics might include:

- A timely report of state-of-the-art analytical techniques
- A bridge between new research results as published in journal articles and a contextual literature review
- A snapshot of a hot or emerging topic
- An in-depth case study or clinical example
- A presentation of core concepts that readers must understand to make independent contributions

SpringerBriefs in Psychology showcase emerging theory, empirical research, and practical application in a wide variety of topics in psychology and related fields. Briefs are characterized by fast, global electronic dissemination, standard publishing contracts, standardized manuscript preparation and formatting guidelines, and expedited production schedules.

Leandro Loriga

Instinct, Reason and the Self in the Aftermath of Postmodernity

Beyond Reason

Springer

Leandro Loriga
Department of Medical Psychology and Ethics, Faculty of Medicine
Masaryk University
Brno, Czech Republic

ISSN 2192-8363 ISSN 2192-8371 (electronic)
SpringerBriefs in Psychology
ISBN 978-3-032-25338-5 ISBN 978-3-032-25339-2 (eBook)
https://doi.org/10.1007/978-3-032-25339-2

This Springer imprint is published by the registered company Springer Nature Switzerland AG
The registered company address is: Gewerbestrasse 11, 6330 Cham, Switzerland

To Jana

Preface

Before engaging in the arguments of this book, it is necessary to explain why this book came to life in the first place. It began with a simple concern: the role of mentorship in a time when it appears increasingly neglected. By mentorship, I mean the capacity of a mentor to recognise the nuances of a pupil—whether latent or explicit—and to cultivate them without force or constraint, allowing them to unfold and mature organically, so that the pupil might indeed become a better version of oneself.

Yet, mentorship itself depends in turn upon something that is becoming unstable: the capacity to orient oneself within a world that still feels coherent and meaningful. When that sense of orientation collapses—when the frameworks that once provided direction dissolve—mentorship itself becomes impossible. One cannot guide another through a landscape one can no longer read. Historically, such orientation was anchored in tradition, while reason functioned as the navigational tool *par excellence* within it—interpreting, justifying, and transmitting inherited frameworks rather than replacing them. From here, two further questions emerged. First, whether under contemporary conditions tradition can still function as the binding framework—as the map—that allows the subject to orient itself at all. Second, whether that historical tool that enabled orientation upon such familiar ground still retains its value once the terrain it relied upon—tradition itself—begins to erode. In other words, whether reason can still operate as the navigational tool once its grounding shifts or once it becomes detached from the traditions that once anchored it.

We are now in the postmodern era—or rather in its aftermath as I will argue—marked by what Jean-François Lyotard called the incredulity toward metanarratives—that is, the collapse of grand explanatory systems rooted in tradition and grounded in observation of the natural world. It is a world shaped by hyperreality, as Jean Baudrillard described; we are surrounded by signs that no longer point to anything real—only to each other. People become anchored not in anything naturally occurring—whether such a ground has ever truly existed lies beyond the present scope—but in reflections of reflections, images detached from substance, increasingly filtered, prioritised, and circulated according to systems that anticipate attention rather than meaning. What appears before us is not what is true or enduring, but what is momentarily salient—that is, what is algorithmically selected and amplified because it stands out, captures attention, and demands engagement—only to dissolve shortly thereafter. In the face of such abundance, clarity disappears. Reason loses its authority as an orienting force; values feel interchangeable, and direction becomes hard to sustain within a social landscape shaped by postmodern exhaustion. Under these conditions, reason can no longer provide a clear direction or shared meaning.

From the Greeks onward, reason was exalted as humanity's defining trait: *logos* was what separated human beings from beasts, granting them the power to order chaos and discern the good. This Western tradition—renewed in the Enlightenment and later systematised under positivism—cast reason as the highest form of freedom: the means by which humankind could rise above instinct, ignorance, and superstition. In this Western narrative, reason becomes not only a tool but also the very symbol of human liberation—from ignorance, from instinct, and from nature itself. But what happens when reason ceases to engage the natural world it once sought to master, and turns instead upon itself—when the meanings once drawn from the very nature humanity sought to escape through reason are rebuilt upon those same man-made constructs? In this self-referential loop, knowledge no longer seeks to understand natural processes, but to elaborate upon its own interpretations—reproducing symbols that refer only to one another. What once served to explain the world now generates a world of its own: copies without originals.

In this book, I seek to trace the path by which reason drifted from its grounding and collapsed into a sea of symbols, that is, signs without reference to what was once thought to be the real. Yet, I do not want to stop here. I wish to take a step further. We are not only in a postmodern era, but rather in its aftermath. After the collapse of tradition and the saturation of symbolic environments, what emerges is what I shall call a *Sensorial Nexus*: a condition in which algorithmic systems no longer merely present information but begin to pre-organise perception itself.

If this diagnosis is correct, the question that follows is whether orientation can be recovered under such conditions. In proposing a way forward, I seek to offer, without presumption of exhaustiveness, a possible glimpse of a way back to meaningful existence—by recovering a mode of orientation grounded in embodied and non-propositional modes of understanding. These are ways of knowing that operate prior to explicit reasoning, concepts, or articulated beliefs and that guide action through felt sense, responsiveness, and attunement rather than argument or justification.

Brno, Czech Republic Leandro Loriga

Competing Interests The author has no competing interests to declare that are relevant to the content of this manuscript.

About the Book

This book is organised into six chapters, each divided into clearly distinguished smaller sections in order to maintain conceptual precision while allowing the central argument to unfold progressively.

Chapter 1: From Tradition to Doubt examines the historical role of tradition as an embodied framework of orientation. It analyses how shared narratives once stabilised meaning, authority, and mentorship and how the gradual elevation of reflective reason introduced structural doubt. What begins as intellectual emancipation ultimately destabilises the inherited ground upon which judgement once rested.

Chapter 2: The Postmodern Era traces the intensification of this destabilisation. Postmodern critique dismantles foundational narratives and exposes the fragility of truth, identity, and coherence. Yet, the collapse of certainty does not produce liberation; it results in fragmentation, performativity, and proliferation of symbolic mediation without stable anchoring.

Chapter 3: Posthumans, Transhumans and the Sensorial Nexus introduces the book's central conceptual contribution: the *Sensorial Nexus*. Building on the diagnosis of postmodern fragmentation, this chapter argues that we now inhabit its operational aftermath, in which digital infrastructure, algorithmic governance, and predictive systems no longer merely circulate representations but organise salience at the level of perception itself. The Sensorial Nexus names a condition in which affect, attention, and relevance are pre-structured prior to reflection, such that judgement increasingly unfolds within environments already engineered for anticipation. What is at stake is not the disappearance of freedom, but the compression of the interval in which deviation, hesitation, and originality can stabilise.

Chapter 4: Beyond Rationalism: Intuition, Habit, and Tacit Orientation defends the philosophical legitimacy of non-propositional modes of knowing. Drawing on Bergson, Hume, and Polanyi, it argues that instinct—understood as intuition, habit, and tacit integration—is not opposed to reason but constitutes its enabling ground. Reason remains indispensable, yet it presupposes a pre-reflective orientation it cannot itself generate.

Chapter 5: From Van Gennep to the DIEM Method: A Contemporary Model of Transformation marks the book's principal practical contribution.

Moving from diagnosis to enactment, it adapts van Gennep's tripartite grammar of separation, liminality, and incorporation into a contemporary framework designed explicitly as resistance to the operations of the Sensorial Nexus. The DIEM method—Disruptio, Introspectio, Examen, Manifestatio—is proposed as a disciplined interruption of algorithmic pre-structuring: a way of suspending engineered salience, dismantling performative identity, reclaiming judgement through radical honesty, and returning to action without surrendering orientation to anticipatory systems.

Chapter 6: The Future After Collapse draws the argument together. It renders the central claim explicit, addresses possible objections, and reflects on the implications of a world in which prediction and optimisation increasingly replace shared meaning. The final question concerns whether judgement and responsibility can still emerge within environments that continuously anticipate and organise response in advance.

Contents

Chapter 1
From Tradition to Doubt

In the opening remarks, I mentioned that this book was born out of a concern with mentorship, which I felt was increasingly neglected in today's Western world. As I started exploring these themes more in depth, another question emerged, one that seemed closer to the root of this neglect. What kind of world are we living in, where mentorship is no longer a natural part of maturing? Earlier, I described our present age as a *postmodern condition*—a time when the traditional tools for navigating life no longer seem to work. But what exactly does this mean? And why does it matter? To answer this, one must first take stock of the landscape we are trying to cross. Because for anyone feeling lost, the very terrain beneath their feet may be part of the problem. We are no longer walking on familiar ground. We are walking through a simulation. At least, this is something that some philosophers might claim. Before confronting the fog of postmodernity directly, however, we must first turn to a concept that once provided direction with remarkable stability: tradition.

1.1 Tradition: Concept and Function

A compelling starting point is to argue that we no longer live in a world where tradition speaks with unquestioned authority. A grandmother's cold remedy is dismissed the moment a Google search or an AI-generated health tip claims a more evidence-based fix. A father's manual know-how—how to fix a loose hinge, mend a chair, or work a piece of wood—is bypassed by a 2-min YouTube tutorial uploaded from the other side of the ocean. Even simple inherited routines are overwritten by whatever trend dominates social media that week, whether a viral tweet, an influencer tip, or a streaming-platform life hack. To understand what has been lost in this pursuit of the perfectly optimised method—whether to look better, succeed faster, or become more efficient and what might still be reclaimed—one needs to look more closely at

L. Loriga, *Instinct, Reason and the Self in the Aftermath of Postmodernity*, SpringerBriefs in Psychology, https://doi.org/10.1007/978-3-032-25339-2_1

what tradition is, how it functions, and what forces have gradually worn it down. This chapter is not a historical overview but a conceptual diagnosis. Even so, it draws on the work of certain historians, such as David Gross (see, e.g. Gross, 1992b), to offer an account of how tradition operates and what happens when it begins to break down.

I will begin by saying that tradition is not something rigid or nostalgic but a living thread that connects us to those who came before. It is less about preserving old habits and more about keeping a conversation alive—one that stretches across generations. The Latin root of the word, *tradere*—David Gross notes—means both *to hand over* and *to entrust* (Gross, 1992a, p. 9). That dual meaning says a lot. Tradition is not just about receiving something old—it is about being trusted to carry it forward, shape it, question it, and even change it when needed. It is a responsibility as much as it is a legacy. So, what exactly counts as a tradition? Not everything old deserves the name. Gross suggests that to be recognised as a tradition, a practice must persist across at least three generations, carry moral or spiritual weight, and offer a sense of continuity with the past. These features distinguish tradition from mere custom. Customs can be superficial, passively inherited, and easily discarded. However, tradition holds a particular kind of authority. It asks for engagement. One does not simply follow a tradition; one converses with it. Tradition, moreover, is not static. Like a riverbed that channels new waters, it changes with time. It is a dialogue. It remains alive only so long as the conversation continues. When a tradition becomes mechanical—when the gestures remain, but the meaning is gone—it begins to die. Importantly, tradition does not always live in official institutions. It can survive underground, kept alive by communities of memory—grandmothers, healers, dissidents. In such cases, tradition becomes not only a guide but a form of resistance. It remembers when everything else forgets.

This living, adaptable force has come under strain. From the early modern period onward, tradition began to face both internal and external challenges (Gross, 1992b). Internally, the growing complexity of society splintered once-unified traditions into smaller, localised versions. These fragments were often inherited without the context that once gave them coherence. What had been embodied knowledge became abstract information. Meanwhile, the way tradition was transmitted began to shift. Oral practices gave way to writing and later to print, radio, and television. The intimate, bodily dimensions of tradition began to slip away.

> *By contrast with natural, oral speech, writing is completely artificial. There is no way to write 'naturally'. Oral speech is fully natural to human beings in the sense that every human being in every culture who is not physiologically or psychologically impaired learns to talk. Talk implements conscious life but it wells up into consciousness out of unconscious depths, though of course with the conscious as well as unconscious cooperation of society. Grammar rules live in the unconscious in the sense that you can know how to use the rules and even how to set up new rules without being able to state what they are.* (Ong, 2002, p. 81)

Where the body once remembered—through dance, prayer, gesture—now only the screen or the page remained. Memory became mediated. Meaning became distant. Externally, tradition was undermined by new ways of knowing. Francis Bacon's empiricism demanded observable, testable knowledge (Bacon, 1902). Descartes' rationalism urged people to trust reason over inherited belief (Descartes, 2010). Tradition, once a source of truth, became a problem to overcome. Charles Taylor, for example, argues that, in modernity, inherited moral and metaphysical traditions lost their status as unquestioned sources of truth and were increasingly treated as problematic systems requiring justification, revision, or rejection.

> *It is now a commonplace about the modern world that it has made these frameworks problematic. On the level of explicit philosophical or theological doctrine, this is dramatically evident. Some traditional frameworks are discredited or downgraded to the status of personal predilection, like the space of fame. Others have ceased to be credible altogether in anything like their original form...* (Taylor, 2000, pp. 16–17)

This marked a profound cultural shift. The modern subject no longer looked backward for guidance but forward for progress. History, once the anchor of identity, became something to be surpassed. The rise of capitalism and the modern state accelerated this process even further. The market valued speed and innovation, not reverence. Bureaucracy, as Max Weber claims, for example, replaced local knowledge with uniform rules—*the need for constant, firm, intensive, and calculable administration was created historically by capitalism—not entirely by capitalism, but undeniably primarily, and cannot exist without it* (Weber, 2019, p. 351). Tradition was not just sidelined—it was systematically displaced.

1.2 Tradition as Lived Order

Borrowing from David Gross, I mentioned that tradition is a living moral inheritance. Before the rise of modernity, people did not question the purpose of tradition. They did not need to. It was already everywhere: in the land, the rituals, the body, the calendar, the law. Meaning was not a question. It was a shared atmosphere. You did not have to seek it—it was embedded in your surroundings, passed on not as an option but as a condition of life.

From the ancient world to the late Middle Ages, tradition was not one source of knowledge among others. It was the whole structure. In these societies, time itself pointed backward. The past was sacred. Origins held authority. The closer something was to the source—to myth, to the ancestors, to the Gods—the more it was trusted (see, e.g. Eliade et al., 2018). To live well was to align with what had already been given. In ancient Athens, for example, civic virtues were transmitted not only through debate but also through participation in festivals, mourning rites, and public rituals. In medieval Europe, the feasts of saints, the agricultural calendar, and even the physical layout of the village were designed to reflect divine order (e.g. Loraux, 2006; Parker, 1996). Tradition governed everything—from harvest cycles to legal codes to moral duties. Myths explained how the world began. Laws reflected cosmic order. Rituals were not quaint customs but enactments of truth. To break from tradition was not just to change—it was to endanger the balance of the world. Even small acts—eating the wrong food during Lent, walking on a forbidden path, or speaking a name aloud—could be seen as dangerous ruptures. Tradition was the immune system of the community.

This reverence for the past persisted throughout the premodern period, encompassing classical antiquity and medieval Europe. But over time, tradition became more structured and embedded. It was institutionalised in the Church, the monarchy, and the family (Gross, 1992a, pp. 20–40). Inherited roles organised life. Identity was not something you chose—it was something you were born into.

> *I define who I am by defining where I speak from, in the family tree, in social space, in the geography of social statuses and functions, in my intimate relations to the ones I love, and also crucially in the space of moral and spiritual orientation within which my most important defining relations are lived out.* (Taylor, 2000, p. 35)

One's name, work, and duty were all embedded in a chain that reached back into the past. To be a blacksmith, a daughter, a peasant, or a monk meant fulfilling a role that came with meaning already attached. The choice was limited, but orientation was strong. Tradition lived in the body. It was carried in the way one knelt, greeted others, prepared food, and marked the seasons. Knowledge was not only transmitted through words but through action, repetition, and ritual (Mauss, 1973). Even when societies grew more complex—through empire, trade, and conquest—tradition continued to adapt. It absorbed differences by reinterpreting them through older forms. Think of how Roman religious rites absorbed foreign Gods by Latinising their names and myths. Or how local saints replaced pagan deities in rural Europe without altering the rituals themselves (Brown, 2007). Tradition was elastic, but its shape remained recognisable.

The early modern period—the fifteenth to seventeenth centuries—introduced something new in the West: fracture. A previously shared cultural order—tradition—no longer functioned as an unquestioned unity. As Peter Burke claims, from the sixteenth century onward, 'there were more frequent attacks on traditional popular culture, and there were more systematic attempts to purge it of both its "paganism" and its "licence"' (Burke, 2026, p. 250) and 'the resilience of popular culture began to break down, and important changes took place' (Burke, 2026, p. 264). What had once been inherited as a living continuum of ritual, feast, custom, and embodied belief was now subjected to critique, reform, and suppression.

This breakdown produced not continuity but conflict and pluralisation. Competing confessional and moral orders—Catholic, Lutheran, Calvinist, and radical reform—now confronted one another across Europe. The unity of belief, custom, and worldview began to crack. People no longer simply inherited one tradition; they increasingly encountered rival systems of meaning. Belief ceased to be self-evident. It became something to be defended, purified, or rejected. The act of believing now required justification.

Philosophy drove this shift further. Francis Bacon explicitly rejected received authority in favour of experiment, insisting that, 'truth is not to be sought in the good fortune of any particular conjuncture of time, which is uncertain, but in the light of nature and experience, which is eternal' (Bacon, 1902, p. 30). Knowledge could no longer rest on inheritance or tradition but had to be reconstructed through method and experiment, 'for truth is rightly named the daughter of time, not of authority' (Bacon, 1902, p. 62).

René Descartes pushed this break further by demanding that belief begin not with inheritance but with methodical doubt.

> *I reject as absolutely false everything in which I could imagine the least doubt, in order to see whether, after this process, something in my beliefs remained that was entirely indubitable... I resolved to pretend that all the things that had ever entered my mind were no more true than the illusions of my dreams.* (Descartes, 2010, p. 18)

Knowledge was no longer grounded in tradition, authority, or the senses but reconstructed from the certainty of the thinking subject alone.

> *"I am, I exist" is necessarily true every time I utter it or conceive it in my mind.* (Descartes, 2010, p. 64)

Tradition thus ceased to be a given—it became something to prove or discard. The old authority of the elders, the Church, and the village was progressively displaced by the authority of the individual mind. The Enlightenment later radicalised this logic. Immanuel Kant famously defined the Enlightenment as mankind's exit from intellectual inheritance:

> *Enlightenment is man's emergence from his self-incurred immaturity. Immaturity is the inability to use one's own understanding without the guidance of another. This immaturity is self-incurred if its cause is not a lack of understanding, but a lack of resolution and courage to use it without the guidance of another. The motto of the Enlightenment is therefore: Sapere Aude! Have courage to use your own understanding!* (Kant, 1991, p. 54)

Knowledge was no longer understood as tradition received but as reason exercised and belief requiring public justification, since 'the public use of man's reason must always be free, and it alone can bring about Enlightenment among men...' (Kant, 1991, p. 55).

Technological change reinforced the transformation. The printing press altered how information was stored, transmitted, and authenticated. Oral wisdom increasingly became textual. Ritual yielded to commentary. People began to read what they had previously lived. What had once been absorbed unconsciously through imitation, repetition, and rhythm was now mediated by interpretation. Scripture replaced gesture. Theory displaced presence (on the shift from orality to textual culture, see Ong, 2002, mentioned above).

Modernity then completed the shift. The industrial economy rewarded speed, not memory—bureaucracies enforced regulation, not tradition. Identity was reshaped by systems—market, nation, ideology—not by ancestral ties. As Max Weber observed:

> *Man is dominated by the making of money, by acquisition as the ultimate purpose of his life. Economic acquisition is no longer subordinated to man as the means for the satisfaction of his material needs.* (Weber, 2013, p. 18)

Factory time replaced sacred time. Efficiency displaced reverence. The past survived in museums and archives—but no longer in daily life. The sacred rhythms of tradition gave way to deadlines, data, and decisions. People still celebrated holidays and wore symbols of faith or heritage—but increasingly as gestures of nostalgia, not shared belief. Tradition no longer defined who we were. It became one of many stories we might tell. It became performative (for a comprehensive account of this historical and epistemic shift, see Gross, 1992b, 2011), something we do to feel rooted, not something that roots us. Modern individuals are born into an economic order that binds them.

> *This order is now bound to the technical and economic conditions of machine production, which today determine the lives of all the individuals who are born into this mechanism, not only those directly concerned with economic acquisition, with irresistible force.* (Weber, 2013, p. 123)

Something was lost in this shift. Tradition offered more than stability—it had offered a framework for meaning, a deep sense of belonging, and a connection to something larger. In stepping away from it, modern life gained autonomy—but perhaps lost coherence. Today, we stand at the edge of that loss. The institutions that replaced tradition—science, reason, the market, the state—no longer offer the sense of order they once promised. The old structures are failing, but nothing clear has taken their place. What emerges in that vacuum is not freedom but fragmentation. And that fragmentation has a name. It is postmodernity.

1.3 Instinct and Reason: A Continuum

So far, I have argued that tradition once offered a stable framework for meaning and that it has been gradually eroded—through the philosophical shifts of early modernity, the rise of rationalism, and the economic and administrative structures of modern capitalism. The previous sections traced this movement from a world organised by inherited certainties to one increasingly marked by fragmentation, a trajectory that will eventually lead to what we now call postmodernity. But before examining postmodernity itself, it is necessary to dwell on a parallel shift that unfolded alongside the erosion of tradition. This shift—epistemic in nature as I argue—concerns how individuals navigated life and its meanings. To trace this development, I introduce two new terms, *instinct* and *reason*, and show how their changing relationship sheds light on the aetiology of postmodernity: the rise of doubt as a dominant structure of experience. The first thing to clarify is what I mean when I speak of instinct and what I mean when I speak of reason; it is necessary to define these two terms in order to make sense of what comes next in this disambiguation.

By *instinct*, I do not mean a fixed biological mechanism or a single, clearly bounded faculty. Nor do I treat it as a concept that can be exhaustively defined without distortion. I deliberately leave the term open. In this book, *instinct* functions as an umbrella term, used to gather insights from different authors and traditions that point toward a shared domain: what I will define broadly as pre-reflective, embodied, and non-propositional modes of orientation. It refers to ways of sensing, responding, and finding one's bearings that precede abstraction, deliberation, and explicit reasoning. In this sense, instinct is closer to what Merleau-Ponty describes as sensibility, understood as 'our means or manner of opening on to a world we are already "in" or "of"' (Cataldi, 2008, p. 163). It is a bodily intentionality, not reducible to animal reflex, but expressive of our situated being-in-the-world' (Merleau-Ponty, 2002). Any attempt at full precision or conceptual closure would repeat the very failure this book seeks to diagnose: the imposition of rational containment on forms of orientation that resist being fully captured by reason without being diminished. Instinct, as used here, remains deliberately open—describable, cultivable, and intelligible, but never exhaustively definable without loss.

When I speak of *reason*, on the other hand, I mean an extension of that same embodied responsiveness into reflection and articulation. Reason, in this sense, operates through propositional modes of orientation: it renders experience into statements, rules, arguments, and explanations that can be named, evaluated, transmitted, and contested. To orient propositionally is to relate to the world through claims—*this is the case, this follows from that, this ought to be done*. Reason translates embodied responsiveness into concepts, categories, and judgements, allowing experience to be stabilised, shared, and systematised. In doing so, it makes orientation codifiable and communicable, but not exhaustive. This contrast does not mark a hierarchy. Reason is not opposed to instinct, nor does it replace it. It extends, refines, and reorganises it. The problem arises only when propositional orientation claims exclusive authority—when what can be stated, justified, or measured is treated as the only legitimate form of knowing.

Instinct and reason, therefore, are not antithetical faculties but complementary dimensions of human life: instinct provides orientation through embodied sensitivity, while reason gives articulation, reflection, and awareness to that sensitivity. This proposition is defensible and finds grounding across philosophy, phenomenology, cognitive science, and evolutionary anthropology. Henri Bergson, for example, describes intelligence (understood here as reason in its propositional, relational, and instrumental form) and instinct as complementary developments of life, arguing that intellect differentiates from instinct rather than breaking from it. Reason, on this view, is not a rupture but a later articulation—an analytical refinement of an older, embodied mode of knowing. As Bergson notes, when discussing the development of animal life, 'intelligence and instinct, having originally been interpenetrating, retain something of their common origin. Neither is ever found in a pure state' (Bergson, 2005a, p. 149). Life, therefore, begins as a single, undivided impulse which, in the course of its expansion, differentiates into divergent tendencies rather than discrete faculties (see, e.g. Bergson, 2005b). Instinct and intelligence are two such tendencies. Instinct develops toward immediate action through the use of organised natural instruments—structures shaped by life for specific functions. Intelligence, by contrast, develops toward indirect action, constructing and varying artificial tools rather than inheriting them. Both stem from the same original vital impulse, but each unfolds by accentuating one tendency at the relative expense of the other. As Bergson argues, instinct involves an innate knowledge of things, whereas intelligence involves an innate grasp of relations—two complementary but divergent modes of knowing rooted in a common source and differentiated through the divergence of life's tendencies.

A good practical example to understand this differentiation is the paralysing wasp, as Bergson describes it. When the wasp seeks a host for its larva, it does not *reason* about anatomy or experiment with possibilities. It stings its prey at the exact points where the nervous centres lie, immobilising it without killing it. As Bergson notes, 'it acts like a learned entomologist and a skilful surgeon rolled into one' (Bergson, 2005a, p. 161). This is instinct: an *immediate*, embodied knowing of a concrete situation—*knowledge of a thing*—expressed directly in action. By contrast, what Bergson calls intelligence operates through relations, not things. It analyses means and ends, imagines alternatives, tests different paths; its knowledge is not given in the act but constructed through reflection. This is why Bergson takes the first stone tools—such as the flint axes identified by Boucher de Perthes—as the earliest unmistakable sign of intelligence. As he puts it:

> *If we could rid ourselves of all pride, if, to define our species, we kept strictly to what the historic and the prehistoric periods show us to be the constant characteristic of man and of intelligence, we should say not Homo sapiens, but Homo faber.* (Bergson, 2005a, p. 153)

Both capacities aim at solving practical problems, but they do so through divergent developments of the same original impulse: instinct acts through inherited precision; intelligence acts through reflective reconstruction.

Evolutionary anthropology further supports this continuity. Michael Tomasello, for example, argues that uniquely human forms of reasoning grow out of prior cooperative instincts: shared attention, imitation, gesture, and joint intentionality (Tomasello, 2001). Language, logic, and conceptual thought emerge because early humans were already attuned to others at an instinctive, embodied level. Rationality is culturally scaffolded, but its foundation lies in evolved dispositions for coordination and cooperation. Reason, therefore, is not a break from instinct but its social elaboration.

> *During early ontogeny... the child comes to experience herself as an intentional agent—that is, a being whose behavioural and attentional strategies are organised by goals—and so she automatically sees other beings with whom she identifies in these same terms. Later in ontogeny, the child comes to experience herself as a mental agent that is, a being with thoughts and beliefs that may differ from those of other people as well as from reality—and so from that time on she will see conspecifics in these new terms.* (Tomasello, 2001, pp. 14–15)

The order is explicit: first, an embodied, instinctive identification with others; then the reflective capacities that grow out of it. Cultural learning, language, and reasoning appear later only because they are scaffolded by this pre-reflective social attunement.

There is no point in continuing to dwell on the continuity between instinct and reason. The proposition itself is not radical; it simply restates a continuity long recognised, from philosophical accounts such as Bergson's to developmental and evolutionary perspectives such as Tomasello's. It functions here as a starting point, not as an extravagant claim. It takes this continuity as the runway for what follows. This position departs from the rationalist tradition outlined earlier in this chapter—from Bacon's rejection of inherited habit, through Descartes's methodical doubt, to Kant's demand for autonomous reason. Instinct is not treated as something to be displaced, but as the ground upon which reason later develops.

1.4 The Birth of Doubt

Instinct and reason, therefore, are not antithetical faculties but two phases of the same continuum: instinct as embodied, pre-reflective orientation, and reason as its later, reflective articulation. Once this reflective capacity emerged and later intensified, a new condition arose: the capacity not merely to act, but to reflect on one's reasons for acting.

Ambardekar, in his analysis of whether reflection improves our epistemic situation—that is, our position with respect to knowing, understanding, or justifying beliefs—defines the capacity to think about one's reasons for acting as *reflective cognition*. In the present framework, this corresponds to reason operating reflexively: propositional orientation turned back upon the agent's own impulses, beliefs, and justifications—the very forms of judgement already introduced earlier (*this is the case*, *this follows from that*, *this ought to be done*).

> *Reflection is defined here as second-order reasoning: reasoning that is guided by second-order considerations about one's beliefs or one's normative reasons for belief.* (Ambardekar, 2024, p. 804)

And again

> *...reflection is a capacity to double-check our unreflective responses to the world, including beliefs and intentions. Reflection—as I understand it—refers to a process of second-order reasoning wherein agents seek to confirm or revise their unreflective responses in light of normative considerations about the reasons for or against those responses.* (Ambardekar, 2024, p. 805)

Think of a pedestrian who, hearing rapid footsteps behind them at night, experiences an immediate surge of vigilance and prepares to bolt across the street and flee. This first reaction is an *unreflective response*—an instinctive orientation toward possible danger. A moment later, however, a second cognitive layer intervenes: the person asks themself whether the sound really signals a threat, considers alternative explanations (a jogger, a neighbour, someone rushing for the bus), and revises their initial impulse accordingly. This shift from acting on a felt impulse to evaluating *whether the impulse is a good reason to act* exemplifies Ambardekar's point. Reflection enables humans to stop and assess their impulses. Ambardekar, drawing on Kornblith's account, cites the latter's formulation:

> *We are capable of reflecting on our beliefs and desires, stopping to assess them, and stopping to question the wisdom and the advisability of further belief or action. When we reflect and when we engage in reflective evaluation of our first-order states, it seems that we bring*

> *to bear certain normative standards on our beliefs and actions in a way that other animals could not possibly do.* (Kornblith, 2012, p. 109)

Reflective cognition is therefore not a detached, metaphysical faculty but a deepening of instinct: an organism turning back upon its own orientations, interrupting them, scrutinising them, and imagining alternatives. This, however, comes at a cost. Once the organism can suspend immediacy—once it can ask *why* it believes or acts—its original adaptive clarity fractures.

The same reflective capacity that allows a human to correct errors also introduces new vulnerabilities. Such capacity can become inert, self-congratulatory, or causally disruptive, shaping belief in the wrong kind of way. This does not amount to a rejection of reflection as such. It points instead to the risk that arises when reflection is carried out in isolation. Reflection proves more effective when embedded in interaction with others—when assumptions can be questioned, challenged, and refined. Reflective judgement, in other words, depends on a social framework capable of correcting individual distortions. The difficulty, then, is clear: what happens when that external framework begins to weaken or destabilise? In a postmodern context—examined in the next chapter—the very structures that once anchored reflective judgement become unreliable, leaving reflection vulnerable to confusion and paralysis. The aetiology of this condition has already been outlined above. In this sense, reflective cognition marks the first decisive widening of the gap between impulse and interpretation. It introduces a new kind of cognitive delay—a reflective pause shaped by second-order evaluation. And once this delay exists, instinctive responsiveness is no longer sovereign. A supervisory mechanism has arisen: reason as an internal observer capable of revising, inhibiting, overriding, or second-guessing the very impulses from which it evolved.

1.5 From Immediacy to Symbolic Mediation

This shift—from immediate, instinctive responsiveness to mediated, symbolically organised one—marks the moment when instinctive immediacy is no longer sovereign. A new layer of cognition appears—one that can hold action in suspension, question its own impulses, and create a gap between stimulus and response. Such a position is, once more, not a radical one.

Terrence Deacon (Deacon, 1998), for example, argues that the emergence of symbolic reference transformed this gap between impulse and action precisely. By *symbolic reference*, Deacon does not mean mere signals, associations, or gestures—a vervet monkey's alarm call, a dog's raised hackles, or a learned association like the ring of a bell equals food ready on the table. These operate through resemblance, correlation, or conditioning. Symbolic reference, instead, refers to a mode of meaning that depends on relationships among symbols themselves. The word *lion*, for instance, does not mean what it does because it resembles a lion or reliably appears in its presence, but because it occupies a position within a structured network of other symbols—*animal*, *predator*, *danger*, *male/female*. Meaning arises from this system of contrasts and conventions, not from any direct sensory cue.

> *Focusing on correspondence alone collapses a multileveled relationship into a simple mapping relationship. It fails to distinguish between the rote understanding of words that my dog possesses and the semantic understanding of them that a normal human speaker exhibits... The correspondence between words and objects is a secondary relationship, subordinate to a web of associative relationships of a quite different sort, which even allows us reference to impossible things.* (Deacon, 1998, p. 70)

Symbolic meaning is determined by its place within a structured network of other symbols, and not by any physical resemblance or causal co-occurrence with what it refers to. It is therefore neither iconic, based on similarity, nor indexical, based on correlation. A portrait is iconic because it resembles a person; smoke is indexical because it correlates with fire. The word *fire*, by contrast, bears no resemblance to flames and need not be physically associated with them. Its meaning derives from convention and from its relations to other words within the symbolic system.

> *In other words, reference itself is hierarchic in structure; more complex forms of reference are built up from Simpler forms. But there is more to this than just increasing complexity. This hierarchical structure is a clue to the relationships between these different modes of reference. Though I may fail to grasp the symbolic reference of a sign, I might still be able to interpret it as an index (i.e., as correlated with something else), and if I also fail to recognise any indexical correspondences, I may still be able to interpret it as an icon (i.e., recognise its re semblance to something else).* (Deacon, 1998, pp. 73–74)

Because more complex processes are built up from simpler ones, symbolic thought extends earlier cognition rather than replacing it; that is, it incorporates perceptual, associative, and instinctive processes into a broader representational framework instead of displacing them. Iconic resemblance and indexical correlation remain operative, but they are reorganised and governed by symbolic relations that allow representations to be combined, contrasted, and projected beyond the immediate present. This symbolic layer introduces a new cognitive architecture in which representational processes can be systematised in ways unavailable to non-symbolic creatures. Once symbols evolve, representational processes no longer track only what is present; they make possible what Deacon calls *extended flights of virtual reference* (Deacon, 1998, p. 458), through which the mind explores possibilities, counterfactuals, imagined outcomes, and non-present relations.

> *Symbolic representation processes have added a new level to this evolution like process. Their power of condensing representational relationships, and supporting extended flights of virtual reference, creates a whole new landscape in which the evolutionary process of mind can wander. By internalising much of the physical trial and error and even internalising abstract models of physical processes that can be extrapolated to their possible and impossible extremes, we are capable of what genetic evolution is not: forethought. Representational processes are the substrate for "final causality," that everyday use of imagined ends to guide the selection of present means. Symbolic processes have freed this process from the bounds of the immediate present and possible.* (Deacon, 1998, pp. 458–459)

Where other animals must test alternatives through action, symbolic creatures can model and revise them internally. This internalisation produces a delay between stimulus and response. Instead of reacting immediately, an organism can suspend action, rehearse alternatives, and evaluate imagined futures. This is what is meant by *forethought modulated by symbols*: the ability for imagined ends to guide present choices.

Symbolic thought thus frees *representational processes* from the immediate here-and-now and enables behaviour guided by scenarios that are not perceptually present. Crucially, this symbolic capacity introduces the same vulnerabilities anticipated earlier: hesitation, self-generated doubt, and instability arising from the proliferation of alternatives once action is no longer anchored in immediacy. Once action can be halted in favour of internal deliberation, hesitation and self-generated doubt naturally increase. Such symbolic systems not only expand interpretive flexibility—creating an ever-growing network of relationships to be navigated, where each symbol gains its meaning from how it contrasts with, combines with, and depends on other symbols—but also introduce a new dimension of instability. This structural openness gives symbolic thought its power, but also its uncertainty.

In this sense, symbolic reference deepens the gap that reflective cognition first opened, extending it from episodic self-monitoring into a stable architecture of representation. Once the mind becomes organised around hypothetical futures, imagined objects, and abstract relations, it becomes capable not only of foresight and planning but also of uncertainty, conflict, and confusion. The symbolic layer adds sophistication, intentionality, and cultural possibility, while simultaneously creating the conditions in which doubt, contradiction, and ambivalence can flourish.

Deacon is not alone in tracing this transition from instinctive immediacy to symbolically mediated thought. Many scholars performed similar exercises in reconstructing the origins of reflective consciousness. Merlin Donald (Donald, 1993) similarly argues that cognition develops through increasingly detached representational stages, culminating in symbolic culture—gesture, language, narrative—which frees thought from the grip of immediate perception, much as in Deacon's account. Symbols make it possible to rehearse scenarios, interrupt automatic reactions, and imagine alternatives before acting. Ian Tattersall (Tattersall, 1998), likewise, treats symbolic thought as a qualitative break rather than a refinement of earlier capacities. Humans alone handle categories, abstractions, and imagined entities—forms of representation that detach behaviour from environmental triggers and require meaning to be worked out rather than perceived. Steven Mithen (Mithen, 2006) adds that once symbolic representations could be combined and transferred across different areas of experience—for example, using social knowledge (understanding of intentions, roles, and relationships) to interpret natural events—thought gained a freedom of movement unavailable to instinctive creatures.

It is not my intention now to rehearse these arguments in a mechanical fashion, for that would turn a carefully developed line of reasoning into a shopping list. The point I am getting at is the following: once consciousness could observe itself, uncertainty entered. The gap between impulse and interpretation widened. As doubt multiplied, culture and language emerged as predictive systems that *serve to stabilise* that uncertainty—a process that gradually replaced lived immediacy with representation. We are now *animals symbolicum* (Cassirer, 2010, p. 26):

> *No longer can man confront reality immediately; he cannot see it, as it were, face to face. Physical reality seems to recede in proportion as man's symbolic activity advances. Instead of dealing with the things themselves man is in a sense constantly conversing with himself. He has so enveloped himself in linguistic forms, in artistic images, in mythical symbols or religious rites that he cannot see or know anything except by the interposition of this artificial medium. His situation is the same in the theoretical as in the practical sphere. Even here man does not live in a world of hard facts, or according to his immediate needs and desires. He lives rather in the midst of imaginary emotions, in hopes and fears, in illusions and disillusions, in his fantasies and dreams. "What disturbs and alarms man," said Epictetus, "are not the things, but his opinions and fancies about the things."* (Cassirer, 2010, p. 25)

Once symbolic activity emerges, the human being no longer encounters the world directly. Symbols mediate everything. Language, art, myth, and religious forms become the lenses through which reality is filtered to the extent that immediacy becomes impossible. What we respond to are not things themselves but the interpretations, expectations, fears, and imagined possibilities generated by our symbolic apparatus. We live surrounded not by raw facts but by meanings—many of them projected, anticipated, or purely imagined. While Cassirer distinguishes *animal rationale* from *animal symbolicum*, the point is that rationality represents only one expression of a much broader symbolic capacity. Myth, art, ritual, and emotionally charged language are not reducible to rational processes; they belong to a symbolic order that exceeds strict logic. What matters, however, is not the taxonomy but the structural role of symbolism itself. Symbolic forms—language, narrative, shared concepts, collective practices—create the cultural framework within which thought becomes organised, stabilised, and transmissible.

Reason is not opposed to symbolism but shaped by it. Rationality develops inside the symbolic forms a culture provides: categories, distinctions, evaluative schemes, explanatory models, and shared interpretive habits. To call humans *animal symbolicum* is therefore to highlight the cultural and symbolic systems that structure experience long before any explicit act of reasoning occurs. When the cultural frameworks that once stabilised these symbolic forms begin to erode, the intrinsic instability of symbolic thought is accentuated, like a pendulum whose swings widen once the external scaffolding that held it steady is removed.

1.6 Conclusion

What this chapter has traced is a double erosion: first, the long historical unravelling of tradition—the gradual loss of inherited frameworks that once anchored meaning, identity, and judgement; second, the emergence of a cognitive architecture in which instinctive immediacy gives way to reflective distance, symbolic mediation, and the widening gap between stimulus and interpretation. These two movements—cultural and cognitive—reinforce one another. As tradition thinned, individuals increasingly relied on reflective judgement to orient themselves; as reflection intensified, doubt multiplied, and the stabilising role of tradition became harder to sustain. Reason, as argued throughout, does not oppose instinct. It grows out of it. But this very extension introduces delay, hesitation, and the possibility of error. Symbolic thought magnifies this further: once meaning is organised through webs of symbols rather than direct cues, orientation depends on interpretive structures that must be learned, shared, and maintained. When those structures falter, uncertainty spreads through the entire system. This is the threshold at which modern reason arrives: reflexive, symbol-saturated, and increasingly detached from the embodied and inherited certainties that once shaped human life. Tradition no longer holds; reason no longer secures; symbolism no longer guarantees coherence. The individual stands before a world in which meaning must be constructed rather than received, interpreted rather than inhabited.

The next chapter begins precisely here, at the point where the threads of this argument converge: the collapse of tradition, the internalisation of doubt, the widening interpretive gap, the growing instability of symbolic mediation. Everything traced so far leads directly into the condition we now call postmodernity. If tradition once provided orientation and reason introduced hesitation, postmodernity radicalises both the erosion of inherited frameworks and the expansion of reflective, symbol-mediated judgement. It marks the moment when the symbolic scaffolding itself becomes unstable—when interpretive frameworks multiply, compete, or dissolve, and when no inherited structure can reliably secure meaning or judgement. Postmodernity is therefore not an academic label, but the lived consequence of the cultural and cognitive shifts examined in this chapter. The next chapter turns to that condition in full. This also prepares the central position of the book. The collapse of reason, as used here, does not mean that reason has vanished or become useless; it means that its long-standing claim to supremacy has reached exhaustion. Modernity entrusted reason with the task of grounding knowledge, securing identity, regulating conduct, and providing orientation in the absence of tradition. But as this chapter has shown, the very structure of reflective and symbolic cognition introduces hesitation, fragmentation, and interpretive drift. Reason became overstretched. It attempted to function not simply as one cognitive tool among others but as the organising centre of human life, and in doing so exposed its own limits. To say that reason has collapsed is therefore to say that it can no longer sustain the authority it once claimed. What follows from this is not a rejection of reason but a reordering. Reason continues to operate—but as one dimension within a broader ecology of human orientation rather than as its sovereign. It must be reintegrated into the embodied, pre-reflective attunement from which it originally emerged. Instinct—understood here once again as an embodied and non-propositional mode of orientation—regains primacy as the basic mode of navigation. Reason, in turn, resumes its natural role: not dictating how to live but clarifying, articulating, and refining the orientations already given in experience. Instinct and reason are not antagonists. They form a continuum whose balance was destabilised when reason attempted to stand alone. Recovering that balance is the argument the book advances and the task the following chapters pursue: to show how this rebalancing can restore orientation in a world saturated with doubt and stripped of inherited certainties.

Bibliography

Ambardekar, P. (2024). On the epistemic value of reflection. *Ergo an Open Access Journal of Philosophy, 11*. https://doi.org/10.3998/ergo.6784

Bacon, F. (1902). *Novum organum* (J. Devey, Ed.). P. F. Collier & Son.

Bergson, H. (2005a). *Creative evolution*. Cosimo Classics.

Bergson, H. (2005b). The divergent directions of the evolution of life. Torpor, Intelligence, Instinct. In *Creative evolution*. Cosimo Classics.

Brown, P. (2007). *The cult of the saints: Its rise and function in Latin Christianity* (Paperback ed., [Nachdr.]). Univ. of Chicago Press.

Burke, P. (2026). *Popular culture in early modern Europe* (4th ed.). Routledge Taylor & Francis Group.

Cassirer, E. (2010). *An essay on man: An introduction to a philosophy of human culture* (46. print). Yale Univ. Press.

Cataldi, S., L. (2008). Affect and sensibility. In R. Diprose & J. Reynolds (Eds), Merleau-Ponty: Key concepts (pp. 163–173). Acumen.

Deacon, T. W. (1998). *The symbolic species: The co-evolution of language and the brain* (1. Publ. As a Norton paperback). Norton.

Descartes, R. (2010). *Discourse on method and meditations on first philosophy* (D. A. Cress, Trans.; 4th ed.). Hackett Publishing Company, Inc.

Donald, M. (1993). *Origins of the modern mind: Three stages in the evolution of culture and cognition* (Nachdr.). Harvard University Press.

Eliade, M., Trask, W. R., & Smith, J. Z. (2018). *The myth of the eternal return: Cosmos and history* (1st ed.). Princeton University Press.

Gross, D. (1992a). *The past in ruins: Tradition and the critique of modernity*. University of Massachusetts Press.

Gross, D. (1992b). Tradition under stress. In *The past in ruins: Tradition and the critique of modernity* (pp. 20–40). University of Massachusetts Press.

Gross, D. (2011). *Lost time: On remembering and forgetting in late modern culture* (1. Print. in paperback). Univ. of Massachusetts Press.

Kant, I. (1991). An answer to the question: 'What is enlightenment? (H. B. Nisbet, Trans.). In H. S. Reiss (Ed.), *Political writings* (2nd ed., pp. 54–60). Cambridge University Press.

Kornblith, H. (2012). *On reflection*. Oxford University Press.

Loraux, N. (2006). *The invention of Athens: The funeral oration in the classical city*. Zone Books; Distributed by the MIT Press.

Mauss, M. (1973). Techniques of the body. *Economy and Society, 2*(1), 70–88. https://doi.org/10.1080/03085147300000003

Merleau-Ponty, M. (2002). The spatiality of one's own body and motility. In *Phenomenology of perception* (pp. 112–171). Routledge.

Mithen, S. (2006). *The prehistory of the mind: A search for the origins of art, religion and science* (Nachdr.). Phoenix.

Ong, W. J. (2002). *Orality and literacy: The technologizing of the word*. Routledge.

Parker, R. (1996). *Athenian religion: A history*. Oxford University Press. https://doi.org/10.1093/oso/9780198149798.001.0001

Tattersall, I. (1998). *Becoming human: Evolution and human uniqueness* (1st ed.). Harcourt Brace.

Taylor, C. (2000). *Sources of the self: The making of the modern identity* (9. print). Harvard Univ. Press

Tomasello, M. (2001). *The cultural origins of human cognition* (3. Printing). Harvard Univ. Press.
Weber, M. (2013). *Protestant ethic and the spirit of capitalism.* Taylor and Francis.
Weber, M. (2019). *Economy and society: A new translation* (K. Tribe, Ed.). Harvard University Press. https://doi.org/10.4159/9780674240827

Chapter 2
The Postmodern Era

The previous chapter traced two intertwined developments: the historical erosion of tradition as a shared source of orientation and the parallel intensification of reflective and symbolic forms of knowing that widened the gap between immediacy and interpretation. What follows is a condition in which reflective judgement is increasingly asked to provide meaning, identity, and direction without the stabilising background that tradition had once supplied. This chapter turns to the condition that emerges from that imbalance. Postmodernity is examined here not as a philosophical doctrine or cultural style, but as a lived configuration of experience in which symbolic mediation becomes unstable, interpretive frameworks proliferate without hierarchy, and orientation itself becomes fragile. It is the point at which doubt ceases to be episodic and becomes ambient; where representation no longer clarifies the world but saturates it; and where meaning is no longer inherited or even coherently constructed, but endlessly deferred, simulated, performed. Before any discussion of reorientation can proceed, the contours of the postmodern condition must be made visible, because it is within this condition that contemporary subjects now attempt to live.

2.1 Postmodernity: Living in the Age of Simulation

Postmodernity is not just a historical moment or an artistic trend; it marks a transformation in how reality is experienced, characterised by the dominance of symbolic representations increasingly detached from embodied experience and inherited meaning. As argued in the previous chapter, symbolic systems are not mere labels attached to reality but relational structures that organise meaning internally, widen the gap between stimulus and interpretation, and detach understanding from immediacy. When the cultural scaffolding that once stabilised these systems erodes,

L. Loriga, *Instinct, Reason and the Self in the Aftermath of Postmodernity*, SpringerBriefs in Psychology, https://doi.org/10.1007/978-3-032-25339-2_2

representation no longer orients experience but begins to drift. The stories that once gave shape and direction to life—religion, nationhood, progress, duty—have frayed or dissolved. In their absence, we are left with fragments: floating images, recycled identities, curated lifestyles, and endless choices.

This condition has been most clearly captured by the French philosopher Jean Baudrillard (1994), who offers a stark diagnosis of our times, in which representation no longer refers to an underlying reality but precedes and produces it. We do not merely inhabit a world mediated by representations; rather, the distinction between reality and representation has collapsed. Representation no longer functions as a means of reference but becomes part of a self-contained system of signs that generates the hyperreal, a *real without origin or referent*. Think of a shop sign in the past: a painted boot meant there was a cobbler inside; a carved loaf meant a bakery. The sign pointed to something real behind it. You entered the shop and met the work, the worker, the object itself. Today, think instead of an influencer profile selling a lifestyle. The image no longer points to a concrete place, craft, or practice you can enter or verify. The sign itself becomes the product. What you consume is the image, not something it transparently refers to. Think again, for example, of René Magritte's famous painting *La trahison des images* (*The Treachery of Images*), which shows a pipe with the sentence '*Ceci n'est pas une pipe*' ('This is not a pipe'). The image resembles a pipe, but it is not one—it merely represents one. The postmodern society moves beyond this insight: we no longer even arrive at the pipe behind the image. The sign no longer refers to an underlying reality at all. It circulates autonomously, replacing reality as the primary point of reference. Baudrillard introduces his theory of simulation through a short parable by Jorge Luis Borges titled *On Exactitude in Science*. In the story, cartographers create a map so perfectly detailed that it eventually becomes as large as the Empire itself they are trying to depict, covering the entire territory. After the Empire collapses, only fragments of the useless map remain scattered across the desert.

> *The territory no longer precedes the map, nor does it survive it. It is nevertheless the map that precedes the territory - precession of simulacra - that engenders the territory, and if one must return to the fable, today it is the territory whose shreds slowly rot across the extent of the map. It is the real, and not the map, whose vestiges persist here and there in the deserts that are no longer those of the Empire, but ours. The desert of the real itself.* (Baudrillard, 1994, p. 3)

In postmodern society, this inversion of map and territory is complete. What we see around us—on screens, in brands, in institutions—is no longer a reflection of something real underneath. It is a copy of a copy, endlessly looping, with no original in sight. This is the precession of simulacra—the replacement of the real by its representation until representation becomes all that exists. There are four stages through which images evolve (Baudrillard, 1994, p. 4):

1. *A faithful reflection of reality—the image is still tethered to something real.*
2. *A distortion of reality—it begins to bend or manipulate the original.*
3. *Masking of the absence of reality—there is no reality left, but the image pretends one still exists.*

4. *A pure simulacrum—the image becomes its own reality, referring only to itself.*

By the time we reach the fourth stage, we are no longer dealing with images that represent anything real. We are surrounded entirely by simulacra—signs that refer only to other signs. This is *hyperreality*: a condition in which the distinction between real and fake, true and false, original and imitation collapses not because it is denied, but because it has become meaningless. Reality is no longer concealed or distorted; it is operationally replaced.

Take media, for instance. News, entertainment, advertising, social media—these are not windows to the world; they construct the world we perceive. Reality shows, for example, do not show people as they are—they show people performing as if they were not being filmed, which becomes the ultimate form of performance. Authenticity itself becomes a curated illusion. Or consider Jean Baudrillard's analysis of Disneyland. He does not treat it as an exception to reality, but as its most accomplished model.

> *Disneyland exists in order to hide that it is the "real" country, all of "real" America that is Disneyland (a bit like prisons are there to hide that it is the social in its entirety, in its banal omnipresence, that is carceral).* (Baudrillard, 1994, p. 10)

Disneyland presents itself as a fantasy so that everything outside it may appear real. But in fact, all of society is governed by the same logic of staged experiences, scripted roles, and recycled narratives. It is not a question of false representation, but 'of concealing the fact that the real is no longer real' (Baudrillard, 1994, p. 10). This same logic extends to politics. Scandals, elections, and televised debates simulate moral engagement while concealing the fact that power itself has become performative. On Watergate, for example—the early-1970s scandal that led President Nixon to resign after being accused of covering up improper political surveillance of the Democratic Party—Baudrillard is explicit: 'Watergate was thus nothing but a lure held out by the system to catch its adversaries - a simulation of scandal for regenerative ends' (Baudrillard, 1994, p. 12). Institutions go through the motions of authority not to exercise it, but to preserve the illusion that it still exists. What is preserved is the image of function, not function itself. Even science, long held as the bastion of objectivity, is not immune. Baudrillard illustrates this logic through the case of the Tasaday people, whose so-called preservation becomes the moment when ethnology itself turns into simulation.

> *In order for ethnology to live, its object must die; by dying, the object takes its revenge for being "discovered" and with its death defies the science that wants to grasp it.* (Baudrillard, 1994, p. 7)

The Tasaday are frozen in an artificial state of authenticity, cut off from contact to preserve the illusion of untouched origin.

> *They become referential simulacra, and science itself has become pure simulation.* (Baudrillard, 1994, p. 7)

What is preserved is no longer a living culture but a manufactured version of it—an authenticity staged for Western observation. In this process, science ceases to uncover reality and instead produces a hyperreal object: more controllable, more legible, and more convincing than the real ever was.

In hyperreality, meaning no longer arises from depth but from circulation. Culture does not develop; it recycles. Trends return, slogans reappear, and identity is enacted rather than inhabited. Action becomes content, and the person a recognisable profile. This is not merely a comment on media saturation or surface culture. It signals a deeper dislocation: a condition in which we act, choose, and even feel as if following a script rather than living a life. Success, happiness, and morality are performed without sustained contact with what they once referred to. It is precisely in such a world that reason loses its orienting force. Choice multiplies, but without anchoring; it becomes endless, paralysing, and unrooted. The problem is no longer how to uncover hidden meanings, but how to live when meaning is no longer given—when it must be forged rather than found. This is the condition of postmodernity: life navigated without a map, surrounded by signs that point everywhere and nowhere. If the inherited tools of orientation—reason and tradition—no longer hold, something else must take their place. It requires an embodied capacity to discern, to resist surface coherence, and to remain oriented without external guarantees.

2.2 Lived Postmodernity: Lifestyle, Performance, Media Saturation, and the Reconfiguration of Experience

Postmodernity, as argued, is an environment that reorganises experience from the inside out. It shapes how individuals inhabit their bodies, construct identities, relate to others, experience time, and generate meaning. It is therefore not best understood as a doctrine that one endorses or rejects, but as an atmosphere—pervasive, ambient, and difficult to escape. Crucially, postmodernity is rarely experienced as rupture. There is no single moment at which individuals recognise that reference has collapsed or that meaning has become unstable. Instead, it is absorbed gradually, through habits, interfaces, routines, and expectations. The shift is phenomenological rather than ideological. What must therefore be analysed is not postmodern theory as such, but postmodernity as a lived condition—one that is embodied, performed, and reproduced in everyday life. A good entry point into lived postmodernity is the concept of lifestyle.

2.2.1 The Codification of Life

Let us start with a bold statement: postmodern societies are marked by a reorganisation of identity, away from production, class, and locality, and toward consumption, choice, and self-presentation. In industrial modernity, work functioned as far more than a means of income. It structured time, anchored moral worth, and located individuals within stable social hierarchies.

> *For most people in these largely working-class areas the future was one defined by a relationship with work and with, for example, the production of coal, or ships or cotton. The people were miners, shipbuilders or mill workers and the basis of social life was for these men and women their relationship with the process of production. Their personal, collective and cultural identities were rooted in the locality around the workplace and in the values of the industry for which they worked.* (Watson, 2011, p. 64)

The collapse of industrial labour, the outsourcing of production, and the *flexibilisation* of employment did not simply change economic arrangements; they dismantled the symbolic frameworks through which people understood who they were. Occupation ceased to function as destiny. Class identity became opaque. The workplace no longer served as a site of collective memory or intergenerational continuity.

> *Lifestyle is a nebulous concept, but most writers agree that the discretionary choices which we make, especially consumer choices, contribute to the construction of our social identities. To a greater or lesser extent we are all defined in the eyes of others by what we buy.* (Watson, 2011, p. 62)

This shift has experiential consequences. Identity is no longer something one *is*, but something one *assembles*. It must be continuously curated, updated, and displayed. Consumption ceases to be instrumental and becomes expressive. Clothing, food, travel, fitness, leisure, and even political commitments function as semiotic resources through which individuals signal belonging, distinction, and aspiration.

Consider the contemporary supermarket or shopping mall as a *cathedral of consumerism* (Watson, 2011, p. 64). These spaces no longer exist merely to distribute goods. They stage experiences. Music, lighting, spatial design, scent, and branding produce an atmosphere in which the act of consumption itself feels meaningful. One does not simply buy food; one participates in a narrative of authenticity, wellness, or ethical awareness. Organic labels, minimalist packaging, and curated aesthetics transform necessities into moral and symbolic statements. What matters here is not deception in the crude sense, but reorientation. Consumption in late modern societies functions as participation in a system of signs rather than the satisfaction of biological needs (Baudrillard, 2012). The object does not refer to utility; it refers to a lifestyle. This logic of lifestyle extends directly to embodiment.

Such a logic does not stop at objects or consumption practices. It extends inward, reshaping how individuals relate to their own bodies.

> *The body itself can be seen as a consumer commodity, and this is a process available and promoted to both men and women. In a competitive world it is not enough to be ordinary and we are all encouraged to approach more nearly the ideal of youthful bodily perfection in order to give ourselves added market value. We may even soon be able to design our children to correspond with our aspirations and pay a surrogate mother to grow the child in order to avoid disruption of career and lifestyle.* (Watson, 2011, p. 65)

The proliferation of cosmetic surgery, fitness regimes, dietary optimisation, wearable technologies, and biohacking practices reflects this shift. The body becomes a site of continuous intervention. Health is redefined as appearance, discipline as visibility. What matters is not how the body feels, but how it looks, measures, and circulates as an image. Individuals increasingly encounter their bodies through screens, metrics, and feedback loops. Step counts, calorie trackers, sleep scores, heart-rate variability, and aesthetic filters translate embodiment into data. What cannot be measured or displayed tends to lose legitimacy. Fatigue, pain, ambiguity, and decline are treated as errors to be corrected rather than conditions to be inhabited.

2.2.2 Metricised Embodiment

Where the body is framed as a consumer object—something to be managed, enhanced, and displayed—this logic does not remain at the level of representation. In the contemporary era of self-tracking, it becomes operationalised in everyday practice. Digital devices, apps, and biometric systems translate bodily states into numbers, transforming lived experience into data to be monitored, compared, and evaluated. As Lupton argues, self-tracking is not a neutral practice of self-knowledge, but a cultural technique that privileges numbers as authoritative forms of truth about the body (Lupton, 2016).

> *[self-tracking] ...encourages people to think about their bodies and their selves through numbers.* (Lupton, 2016, p. 91)

This means that how one feels increasingly matters less than what the device records. For example, a person may feel rested upon waking yet experience anxiety or self-doubt when a sleep-tracking app reports insufficient *deep sleep*, leading them to distrust their own bodily perception in favour of the metric.

> *The data appeared to offer certainty, while the body's perceptions are represented as untrustworthy, inexact, inaccurately mediated through human experience rather than being objective. In these representations, technology and the data it produces are portrayed as offering unique insights into the workings of the human body that individuals' unmediated haptic sensations cannot. Like other biometric technologies, self-tracking devices are viewed as able to peer inside the body, releasing its secrets. These self-tracking discourses therefore fit into a broader understanding of the body, which has been articulated in medicine since the development of visualising and scanning technologies and the use of numerical data to define medical risk and to make diagnoses.* (Lupton, 2016, p. 87)

The optimisation of the body is no longer pursued only through visible consumption—fitness regimes, cosmetic procedures, dietary products—but through continuous measurement and comparison. This is the *metricisation*: the conversion of complex bodily processes into numbers that can be tracked, compared, and evaluated. Metricisation does not replace consumption but embeds it within daily routines, turning ordinary activities—walking, eating, sleeping—into ongoing sites of assessment. It is the *lure of numbers* (Lupton, 2016, pp. 88–92), whereby metrics promise objectivity, precision, and control. Step counts, calorie deficits, heart-rate variability, or sleep scores appear to offer an unmediated access to bodily truth, even when they simplify or distort lived complexity. For instance, a fixed step target (such as 10,000 steps per day) functions as a universal benchmark, irrespective of age, health status, or bodily capacity, encouraging comparison rather than contextual understanding. Singularly enough, this process does not restore a closer relationship to the body. On the contrary, it intensifies distance. Sensation, fatigue, pleasure, and discomfort are subordinated to numerical representations that claim greater authority than lived experience itself. Individuals learn to distrust how they feel in favour of what the data reports. Technology is pushing self-tracker narratives that often report anxiety, guilt, or self-blame when their numbers fall short of targets, even when their subjective well-being feels unchanged. This is particularly evident in cases where individuals continue to exercise, restrict food intake, or override fatigue because the data indicates insufficient activity or caloric deficit. Numbers have moral meanings because they are linked to bodily containment:

> *Bodily containment is linked to moral meanings associated with binary oppositions such as thin/fat, healthy/ill and normal/pathological. The body that is unable to be contained, over which its owner seems to have little control, is an object of pity, ridicule and disgust. In contrast the tightly contained body, associated with a lean and fit body shape, good health and vigour, is portrayed and regarded as ideal and morally just.* (Lupton, 2016, p. 51)

In this sense, self-tracking technologies do not deepen embodiment; they reorganise it around external standards of performance and risk. This is biopower made evident, promoting self-regulation and self-monitoring rather than bodily attunement. The body is treated as something to be managed, regulated, and disciplined through continuous feedback and comparison. Corporate wellness programmes that reward step counts or penalise inactivity through insurance premiums exemplify this shift from external surveillance to internalised self-discipline. This dynamic aligns with the previously proposed idea that postmodern identity is assembled through signs rather than grounded in stable practices or inherited roles. Metrics function as signs of virtue within a wider economy of lifestyle display, where health, discipline, and responsibility must be demonstrated rather than assumed (Ajana, 2013). To be seen as healthy increasingly means to be able to present numerical evidence of compliance, whether through step counts, calorie deficits, or sleep scores.

Btihaj Ajana offers another compelling analysis on how biometrics acts at a structural level. Biometric systems shift identity away from narrative continuity toward measurable markers—a move from the *biographical story* to *bio-digital samples* as the basis of identification.

> *These issues relate mainly to the paradigmatic shift from the biographical story (which for so long has been the means by which an asylum application is assessed) to bio-digital samples (which are now the basis for managing and controlling the identities of asylum applicants). Such purging of identity from the narrative dimension lies at the core of biometric technology's overzealous aspiration to accuracy, precision and objectivity, and raises some of the most pressing bioethical questions vis-à-vis the realm of identification.* (Ajana, 2013, pp. 9–10)

Self-tracking thus represents not a departure from postmodern consumer culture, but its intensification. The body is fully absorbed into the logic of lifestyle: continuously curated, publicly intelligible, and permanently unfinished. Individuals relate to their own embodiment as something to be monitored, optimised, and judged, both by themselves and by others.

> *...establishing sameness of body is a paramount preoccupation of biometric technology. And to fulfil this task, the body is turned into an informational object, a readable text (or rather palimpsest) for statistical (re)measurements and data storage.* (Ajana, 2013, p. 90)

What is lived is not bodily autonomy, but a form of structural self-objectification. The result is a form of alienated embodiment. Individuals see themselves constantly yet feel themselves less. The body becomes externalised—something to be worked on, evaluated, and compared. This is not narcissism in the classical sense; it is structural self-objectification. The subject relates to its own body as to an object in a marketplace.

2.2.3 Performance as Generalised Subjectivity

This reconfiguration of embodiment cannot be understood without addressing the rise of performance as a generalised mode of subjectivity. Susan Melrose (2011), for example, argues that postmodernity dissolves the boundary between aesthetic performance and everyday life. Performance ceases to be an activity one occasionally undertakes and becomes a paradigm through which subjectivity itself is organised. In this sense, performance is no longer restricted to theatres, galleries, or explicitly artistic settings. It becomes a way in which action, identity, and meaning are organised across ordinary social situations. What defines performance here is not theatricality, but the fact that action takes place in time, is oriented toward others, and is exposed to judgement.

> *Performance, 'post-' and 'post-post-', continues to take its place and time as complex action, bound-in to and orientated to spectating...* (Melrose, 2011, p. 198)

Take a job interview as a practical example to illustrate the idea. The candidate is not simply reporting who they are; they are performing competence in real time. Posture, tone of voice, pacing of answers, emotional regulation, and responsiveness are evaluated by an interviewer who occupies the position of spectator and judge. What matters is not a stable inner identity, but how effectively one acts under observation.

A first date arranged through a dating app follows the same performative logic. The encounter is framed in advance by profiles, images, and brief textual cues that establish expectations before the meeting even begins. When the date takes place, the individual is not simply *being themselves*—at least we can safely assume not all the time—but actively performing desirability in real time. Choices of clothing, conversational topics, humour, emotional disclosure, and bodily comportment are continuously adjusted in response to the other person's reactions. Silences, gestures, and timing acquire evaluative weight. As in an interview, the other person functions as both participant and spectator, assessing compatibility, confidence, and affective fit. What determines the outcome is not an inner essence of the subject, but how effectively one enacts attractiveness and social competence under observation.

In lived terms, this means that identity is increasingly enacted rather than inhabited. Social roles are no longer stable positions but ongoing performances. Individuals are expected to be adaptable, expressive, and legible. The subject must be continuously articulated to others—through speech, appearance, online presence, and affect.

> *They take as their target 'the mind', rather than the live spectator, willingly positioned in a performance space and time, of which they are in part constitutive.* (Melrose, 2011, pp. 195–196)

This means that action is not primarily directed toward an abstract inner cognition or private intention, but toward a shared situation in which others are present, watching, and responding. What matters is not what one thinks internally, but how action unfolds in time and space in relation to those who witness it. Meaning is generated through exposure and response, not through detached reflection. This relational structure appears in ordinary situations, such as speaking in a meeting. One does not simply express a thought; one calibrates language, confidence, humour, or restraint depending on who is present and how one expects to be evaluated. The presence of an audience—explicit or implicit—shapes the action itself.

Digital platforms intensify this condition. Social media profiles, dating apps, professional networking sites, and even workplace dashboards require individuals to condense themselves into recognisable formats. Short texts, images, metrics, and badges function as performative acts designed for rapid evaluation. Identity becomes modular: editable, reversible, and optimised for visibility.

> *Naming itself is a word game, rather than a straightforward reference to the way things are.* (Melrose, 2011, p. 194)

Think of a LinkedIn profile or dating app bio. Job titles, personal descriptors, and identity labels do not merely describe a person; they actively perform them. These labels are revised when they stop producing the desired response, much like a performance adjusted after a poor reception. This has temporal consequences. Performances are oriented toward immediacy rather than continuity. Past commitments do not bind the present. Consistency is optional; reinvention is rewarded. What matters is not coherence over time but relevance in the moment. The question *Who are you?* gives way to *What performs now?* This can be seen in how people shift tone, values, and self-presentation across contexts without experiencing this as a contradiction. The same person may perform efficiency and neutrality at work, irony online, and emotional openness in private messages. These shifts are experienced not as hypocrisy but as situational competence.

An important remark must be made now to avoid the accusation of clumsiness: performance is not falsehood. It is not pretending to be what one is not. It is the condition under which there is no stable distinction between acting and being. One becomes what one performs. Performance does not erase the subject. Even in fragmented or technologically mediated contexts.

> *A spectatorial drive to identify and/or constitute indices of the human Self remains, whether or not as spectators one attributes that selfhood to performer or directorial figure or function, regardless of the accusation that such a quest binds the quester unwittingly in, to a tradition of self-referentiality.* (Melrose, 2011, p. 199)

Performance, therefore, does not replace being with appearance; it is the site in which being is continually negotiated under conditions of visibility and judgement.

2.2.4 Media Saturation and Affective Erosion

The performative organisation of subjectivity is further intensified by the saturation of everyday life with media. Events no longer arrive as discrete occurrences to be interpreted after the fact, but as immediately mediated phenomena, shaped in real time by formats of visibility, circulation, and attention. In this environment, representation does not follow reality; it actively structures how events are experienced as they unfold. This dynamic has been examined in analyses of postmodern popular culture, which show how performative subjectivity is normalised and amplified through media forms. John Storey (2011) argues, for example—drawing on Baudrillard (1994) and Fredric Jameson (2005)—that postmodern popular culture no longer merely represents reality but actively produces it.

> *In the hyperreal world of the postmodern, there is no longer a clear distinction between a 'real' event and its media representation. In the same way, O. J. Simpson's trial cannot be neatly separated into a 'real' event that television then represented as a media event. Anyone who watched the proceedings unfold on TV knows that the trial was conducted at least as much for the television audience as it was for those present in the court. Without the presence of the cameras, this would have been a very different event indeed.* (Storey, 2011, p. 206)

News, entertainment, advertising, tragedy, and humour circulate within the same symbolic economy. Catastrophe appears alongside memes, war footage alongside lifestyle content. Events do not demand sustained engagement; they demand attention. Consider contemporary warfare. Conflicts such as the war in Ukraine are not only fought materially but processed symbolically through livestreams, short videos, music overlays, and algorithmic amplification. Each atrocity acquires a thumbnail, a soundtrack, and a lifespan. Suffering becomes content. The event is real, but its mode of appearance is aestheticised. The result is not indifference but affective overload. Individuals are exposed to unprecedented volumes of moral claims, images of suffering, and calls to action, yet experience increasing numbness. Tragedies provoke gestures—hashtags, profile changes, brief expressions of outrage—before attention moves on. Repeated exposure does not necessarily deepen moral understanding but rather may instead erode moral response (Sontag, 2003). The argument here is not that people become immoral through exposure, but that repeated visual exposure to suffering tends to dull moral response rather than deepen understanding. Images shock at first, then risk becoming familiar, consumable, and emotionally blunted. Without narrative, context, or action, spectatorship replaces ethical engagement.

2.2.5 *Performativity and the Technological Reorganisation of Reason*

The lived transformations described so far do not arise solely from cultural change or symbolic saturation. They are accelerated and stabilised by a deeper transformation in how knowledge itself is organised. With the rise of computer-mediated systems, reasoning is increasingly subordinated to criteria of speed, efficiency, and performance rather than truth, justification, or meaning.

> *Computer-mediated communications replace language as the vehicle of reason with information measured according to its effects. In other words, the postmodern condition is effected by a technology that harnesses language for quantitative evaluation, so that it is no longer determined by universal ideals (truth, the just society, freedom, etc.), but rather by local imperatives ('re: figures – my desk, tomorrow'; divert resources from failing department, progress this project, etc.), subject only to the law of increased efficiency.* (Hamilton, 2011, p. 102)

What is described here is a shift in how reasoning itself operates. Language no longer functions primarily as a medium for argument, justification, or shared understanding. Instead, it is increasingly used as a tool for coordination, execution, and optimisation. Statements are valued not for whether they are true or meaningful, but for whether they *produce the desired effect*—whether they move a process forward, trigger an action, or improve performance metrics. A practical example is organisational communication.

An email stating 'RE: figures – my desk, tomorrow' does not argue, explain, or justify; it issues a directive whose success is measured solely by compliance and speed. The content of the figures, their broader significance, or their ethical implications are secondary to whether the task is completed efficiently. Language here functions instrumentally, not deliberatively. What is lost in this transformation is not rationality itself, but orientation: knowledge increasingly answers the question of *how to act* while leaving the question of *why* unresolved.

Rather than treating postmodernism as a purely cultural or discursive mood, it is explicitly tied to *the technological transformation of knowledge itself*, particularly through computerisation and information processing.

> *The production of proof, which is in principle only part of an argumentation process designed to win agreement from the addressees of scientific messages, thus falls under the control of another language game, in which the goal is no longer truth, but performativity - that is, the best possible input/output equation.* (Lyotard, 2005, p. 46)

Knowledge is no longer evaluated according to its truth-content, explanatory depth, or correspondence with reality, but according to its operational effectiveness—its speed, efficiency, and capacity to produce results within a system. This does not mean that reason collapses. On the contrary, rationality intensifies. Everything can be measured, optimised, predicted, and automated. Knowledge becomes instrumental rather than existential. It tells us how, but no longer why.

Lyotard's diagnosis of *incredulity toward metanarratives* captures this condition (Lyotard, 2005, p. xxiv). Shared frameworks of meaning—religion, progress, science, emancipation—lose their authority. This collapse is not merely ideological or cultural but technologically effected: metanarratives erode because language itself is subordinated to performative, computerised imperatives rather than universal ideals. Individuals are left to generate meaning locally, temporarily, and privately, without criteria that endure. Choice proliferates, but direction evaporates.

Take, for example, contemporary algorithmic decision systems. Credit scoring, hiring filters, or content recommendation engines do not ask whether a judgement is *true* or *just* in any substantive sense; they ask whether it performs—whether it predicts behaviour, maximises engagement, or reduces risk.

The next section introduces a new variable into this condition: Artificial Intelligence (AI). If postmodernity hollowed out experience by saturating it with images, simulations, and performances, AI automates this process entirely. The question that follows is no longer how humans perform identity and meaning, but what happens when performance itself no longer requires human presence at all—when simulation becomes autonomous and the postmodern condition enters a transhuman phase.

2.3 Artificial Intelligence (AI) and the Postmodern Conjuncture

Up to this point, I have argued that postmodernity is not merely an intellectual stance but a structural condition shaping how meaning operates in lived reality. The erosion of grand narratives, the destabilisation of truth, and the displacement of reason by performance and affect have transformed knowledge from something grounded to something circulated. Meaning no longer rests on foundations but emerges through use, visibility, and repetition. Judgement becomes provisional, contextual, and increasingly outsourced. In this postmodern landscape, another singular development must now be addressed: the advent of Artificial Intelligence (AI).

Before continuing, a clarification is required. In what follows, Artificial Intelligence (AI) does not refer to automation or computational systems in general nor solely to visible interactive tools such as chatbots or language models. Rather, it designates a broader configuration of algorithmic systems that operate across two interconnected layers. At one level, AI appears as an interface: systems that communicate with users, generate language, frame options, and participate directly in processes of judgement and interpretation. At another level, AI functions as an infrastructural logic: predictive, classificatory, and optimisation systems that operate largely in the background, shaping what becomes visible, relevant, or actionable before conscious deliberation occurs. These layers are inseparable. Interactive encounters with AI are always conditioned by underlying systems that anticipate behaviour, rank possibilities, and modulate attention. The focus of this chapter is therefore not AI as a technical artefact or efficiency tool, but AI as a mediating environment—one that increasingly reorganises meaning, judgement, and orientation as they are lived and experienced by human subjects.

The emergence of AI does not occur in a conceptual vacuum but unfolds within a cultural condition already characterised by epistemic fragmentation and the erosion of stable meaning. AI enters a world in which truth is provisional, judgement is contextual, and legitimacy is increasingly performative rather than grounded. The widespread influence of AI is by now undeniable, and its diffusion is not limited to technical or expert domains. Public participation actively contributes to shaping this new technological phase, particularly through narrative interaction, social engagement, and everyday use. AI systems increasingly function as interfaces for public involvement rather than as neutral background tools (see, e.g. Marmolejo-Ramos et al., 2022). This means that AI does not merely process data behind the scenes, but actively structures how people participate, express opinions, and are incorporated into decision-making processes. In this context, AI becomes the medium through which engagement occurs: collecting narratives, organising viewpoints, and enabling deliberation at scale. This shift is significant because mediation replaces foundations: participation is no longer grounded in stable procedures or shared criteria but is shaped by platforms that organise visibility, relevance, and legitimacy in real time. At the same time, public perception of AI reveals a complex mixture of optimism, anxiety, and instrumental acceptance. In a 2024 large-scale cross-national study (Seth, 2024), public perception of AI was analysed using survey data from 10,000 respondents across 10 countries. The study showed that public attitudes toward AI are neither uniformly positive nor negative, but characterised by simultaneous optimism, anxiety, and pragmatic acceptance. Further studies (e.g. Yigitcanlar et al., 2024) support this view; attitudes toward AI are shaped less by direct technical understanding than by trust, visibility, and perceived social impact, confirming that AI is culturally mediated rather than technologically neutral.

> *One of the challenges for the public to form a clear opinion on AI technologies is that these technologies are an invisible element of daily life, mostly driven by proprietary algorithms. AI technologies are difficult for most people to understand, and hence hard for the public to form a clear and accurate opinion on their opportunities and constraints.* (Yigitcanlar et al., 2024, p. 834)

As historical conditions change, so too does collective sensibility. Technological shifts are interpreted through the dominant cultural frameworks of their time. For many observers, the present moment is increasingly described as the *Fourth Industrial Revolution*, characterised by the exponential expansion of digital, algorithmic, and automated systems into everyday life (Ross & Maynard, 2021; Schwab, 2016). Rather than representing a continuation of earlier phases of industrial modernity, this period is defined by a qualitative shift in the nature of technological change.

> *Now, a Fourth Industrial Revolution is building on the Third, the digital revolution that has been occurring since the middle of the last century. It is characterised by a fusion of technologies that is blurring the lines between the physical, digital, and biological spheres.* (Schwab, 2016, p. 1)

The distinctiveness of this revolution lies not only in the technologies involved but also in their speed, scope, and systemic impact. Contemporary technological breakthroughs are unfolding "at an exponential rather than a linear pace" and are "disrupting almost every industry in every country", producing transformations that extend beyond tools and markets to entire systems of production, governance, and social organisation (Schwab, 2016). In this sense, the Fourth Industrial Revolution is not simply technological but structural, reshaping how societies function at a foundational level.

Before moving on, a clarification is needed as to why AI is introduced in a chapter devoted to postmodernism. AI represents a historically singular development: the first technological transformation to unfold not within a stable epistemic framework, but in the aftermath of its collapse. Earlier technological revolutions—from the printing press to mechanisation, electrification, and computation—emerged in contexts that still presupposed rational subjects, grounded judgement, and shared criteria of truth. AI does not. It arrives in a cultural landscape already shaped by simulation, performativity, and the erosion of epistemic foundations. Rather than challenging these conditions, it operationalises them. Contextuality, plurality, indeterminacy, and the collapse of representation—once philosophical diagnoses—become technical features. This conjunction is unprecedented. AI does not merely follow postmodernity; it accelerates it, adding momentum to a condition already marked by the loss of orientation.

This convergence—that is, the convergence between postmodern accounts of meaning and the formal treatment of language in AI systems—was articulated already in early theoretical reflections on AI. John Hooker, already back in 1999 (Hooker, 1999), identified a structural tension at the heart of AI: the attempt to formalise linguistic activity presupposes a conception of meaning that postmodern philosophy had already rendered untenable. The claim here was not that machines cannot act, calculate, or respond, but that formal systems rely on an implicit theory of language in which meaning is assumed to be definable, rule-governed, and transferable. Against this assumption is the argument that meaning does not arise from formal representation or predefined structures. Rather, meaning emerges only through use, through context-bound interaction, and through participation in shared linguistic practices. Language does not function by encoding stable contents that can be extracted and manipulated independently of practice.

> *The task of writing precise rules for understanding language, then, incurs both a theoretical and a practical difficulty. The theoretical problem is that if such rules could precisely capture the meaning of language, they would constitute a set of definitions. But language does not and cannot receive meaning through definitions. Its meaning is inherent in the shifting and complex patterns of linguistic behaviour that people actually exhibit. The practical problem is that even if one were content to approximate the meaning of language by trying to write rules for appropriate linguistic behaviour, he undertakes a herculean task. I cannot*

> *say outright that it is impossible, and I will consider this issue presently. But it is a mistake to suppose that it is possible because words acquire meaning through definitions that can be formulated as rules for understanding language.* (Hooker, 1999, p. 10)

If meaning is practice-bound rather than rule-based, then any system that operates by manipulating symbols according to predefined structures necessarily treats language as detached from the conditions that make it meaningful. Such systems may reproduce patterns of linguistic behaviour, but they do so by exploiting regularities rather than by participating in the practices from which meaning arises. In other words, this means that understanding language is not a matter of applying rules, but of knowing how to act appropriately within a situation. The same word or expression can be correct, incorrect, ironic, or offensive depending on context, timing, and shared expectations. These judgements cannot be derived from definitions alone but emerge through participation in social practices.

Such a position aligns with postmodern accounts of language and knowledge that reject representational theories of meaning in favour of contextual and performative models. As argued earlier, the erosion of tradition and grand narratives dissolved shared frameworks through which meaning was once stabilised, leaving meaning increasingly dependent on use, visibility, and situational enactment. Meaning, on this view, is not stored, encoded, or transmitted; it is enacted. It exists only within ongoing patterns of use and cannot be stabilised independently of them.

I propose—deliberately and provocatively—that AI represents a second-order abstraction of language, following the earlier postmodern erosion of tradition and shared frameworks of meaning. AI does not overcome this displacement of foundations; it presupposes and intensifies it. By operationalising language as data and treating meaning as an effect of patterned use, AI systems extract language from the already weakened contexts of tradition and re-embed it within technical systems. What was first loosened by postmodernity is now reorganised at a further level of abstraction. In this sense, AI systems enact—often implicitly—the very conditions postmodern theory had already described. The relevance for the present argument is clear. AI does not arrive as a neutral technological development within a stable epistemic world. It emerges within, and reinforces, a postmodern condition in which meaning has already been decoupled from grounding, authority, and reference. AI functions effectively precisely because meaning has become operational rather than referential, performative rather than foundational. It builds upon the prior erosion of shared sense and carries it forward into automated and scalable forms. What this account identified as a structural limitation was not resolved by later developments. It was bypassed. Rather than grounding meaning, contemporary systems approximate it statistically, relying on scale, repetition, and correlation rather than definition or reference.

2.3.1 Large Language Models and the Second Abstraction of Meaning

One might object at this point that contemporary AI no longer relies on the formal conception of meaning criticised above. In particular, large language models (LLMs) do not attempt to define meaning through explicit semantic rules or predefined representations. Instead, they are trained through exposure to massive corpora of textbooks, websites, social media, and other digitised sources—learning statistical regularities of language use rather than deductive rules for correct meaning. On this view, the difficulty identified in formal approaches appears to be bypassed rather than confronted. Meaning is no longer stabilised through explicit definitions or rule-based structures but approximated through patterns of use extracted from large-scale linguistic data. However, this shift does not resolve the underlying problem. While explicit formalisation is abandoned, participation in linguistic practice is not recovered. Large language models do not engage in context-bound interaction, shared forms of life, or situated judgement. They operate on language that has already been detached from the conditions that make it meaningful. What is learned is not meaning as enacted, but statistical regularity extracted from language after its grounding in practice has been eroded.

> *[AI systems] ...are not trained on tidy datasets but on the digital sediment of civilisation, terabytes of text, images, and code.* (Cowans, 2025, p. 1)

Their outputs do not represent beliefs, explanations, or interpretations. They represent proximity to prior patterns. However, this shift does not resolve the problem identified earlier—the problem that meaning cannot be grounded in rules or representations detached from linguistic practice; it merely bypasses it. While explicit rules are abandoned, participation in linguistic practice is not recovered. The model does not engage in context-bound interaction or shared forms of life. Instead, it operates on language already detached from those conditions. What is learned is not meaning as enacted, but statistical regularity extracted from language after its grounding in practice has been eroded. Seen in this light, large-scale AI systems therefore exemplify a second-order abstraction of language. Postmodernity loosened meaning from tradition and shared frameworks; AI systems reorganise what remains once that loosening has occurred. Language is not returned to use but abstracted again—this time into technical systems that treat prior usage as raw material.

This development also marks a shift in inference itself. At the level of subjectivity, the consequences are greater still. AI no longer functions merely as an external instrument but increasingly as a co-producer of cognition itself. Francesco Branda suggests the idea of *generated human* (Branda, 2025)—a subject whose judgements co-evolve with algorithmic outputs rather than being formed independently of them. The central concern here is not whether machines think, but whether humans continue to regard thinking—reflection, hesitation, judgement—as necessary:

> *The question is no longer whether AI is capable of thinking, but whether humans will continue to believe that thinking is necessary.* (Branda, 2025, p. 1)

In such conditions, validation begins to replace reflection. Speed displaces deliberation. Judgement risks being reduced to compliance with synthetically generated suggestions. Branda's examples from healthcare and education are illustrative: clinicians and students increasingly encounter outputs that arrive already framed as answers, encouraging acceptance rather than interrogation. What is eroded is epistemic autonomy—the capacity to pause, doubt, and judge—rather than technical competence. This erosion is not accidental. It follows from a cultural condition already shaped by postmodernity, in which foundations were destabilised and contingency normalised. When shared criteria of meaning and authority have already been weakened, systems that generate fluent responses without grounding encounter little resistance. The habit of deferring judgement precedes the technology that now accelerates it. From a postmodern perspective, AI appears at first to embody familiar motifs: pluralism, contextuality, decentralisation. Contemporary AI systems generate multiple responses, adapt dynamically to situational inputs, and operate without recourse to fixed or authoritative truths, thereby echoing postmodern critiques of representation, certainty, and epistemic hierarchy.

> *These systems adapt to the environment in which they operate, allowing them to offer multiple and varied solutions in line with different perspectives, which fully reflects the principle of pluralism in postmodern thought.... AI deals with a variety of data, and does not rely on fixed central structures, reflecting a postmodern vision that rejects absolute power.* (Alkhazaleh et al., 2025, p. 56)

Yet this apparent alignment conceals an asymmetry. While meanings multiply at the surface, the mechanisms that produce them become increasingly inaccessible. Interpretation proliferates, but control migrates—from discourse to infrastructure, from argument to system design.

This asymmetry becomes clearer when viewed through the lens of virtualisation (Dobrodum et al., 2024). *Virtualisation* refers to the process by which cultural and religious phenomena are increasingly mediated, simulated, and reconfigured through digital systems, producing a blurring of established ontological distinctions. If indeed postmodernity is characterised by the erosion of boundaries '...between the real and the fictional, between fact and fiction, between the sacred and the profane' (Dobrodum et al., 2024, p. 1), then AI plays a central role in accelerating this process. Here, AI is not merely a representational technology. It is capable of *model[ling], analyz[ing], interpret[ing] and transform[ing] cultural and religious phenomena* (Dobrodum et al., 2024, p. 1), thereby influencing language, symbolism, mythology, ethics, aesthetics, identity, values, freedom, and responsibility. Virtualisation, in this sense, refers to the displacement of cultural practices from embodied, situational contexts into technically mediated environments where symbols, rituals, and meanings continue to circulate independently of presence. This process enables continuity under conditions of disruption. Cultural and religious practices persist online; symbols remain accessible; participation is maintained despite physical absence. At the same time, virtualisation introduces a deeper abstraction. Meaning becomes increasingly detached from lived enactment, as practices endure without presence and symbols circulate without grounding. What emerges is not the disappearance of culture or religion, but their transformation into mediated forms whose ontological status becomes ambiguous. The danger here is ontological confusion: a condition in which representation is mistaken for participation, simulation for experience, and mediated fluency for understanding.

2.4 Conclusion

This chapter has examined postmodernity not as a theoretical posture but as a lived historical condition. It has shown how the erosion of tradition, the collapse of reference, and the saturation of experience by representation reorganise meaning, identity, embodiment, and judgement. Drawing on analyses of simulation, lifestyle, performance, popular culture, and technological rationality, the chapter traced how meaning becomes provisional and circulated rather than grounded, how identity is assembled through signs rather than inhabited, and how judgement is displaced by visibility, optimisation, and effect.

Within this already destabilised landscape, the emergence of AI marks a qualitative shift. AI does not arrive as a neutral instrument within a stable epistemic order. It unfolds within a postmodern condition that has already dismantled the foundations of truth, authority, and reason. What postmodernity loosened philosophically, AI operationalises technically. Meaning is no longer interpreted but approximated; judgement is no longer exercised but increasingly deferred; orientation is no longer sought but supplied.

Taken together, these developments point to a condition of historical singularity. We are living at a moment in which:

1. Postmodernity dismantled epistemic foundations such as truth, reason, and authority.
2. Artificial Intelligence operationalises this dismantling at scale.
3. Judgement, already weakened philosophically, is now threatened technically.

This is not simply a continuation of postmodernity. It is its technological afterlife. AI does not restore meaning after postmodernism; it exploits the vacuum postmodernism created. Relativism becomes computation, performativity becomes automation, and fragmentation becomes ambient guidance. Instinct, orientation, and decision-making risk being shaped by systems that neither understand nor doubt.

It is at this threshold that a new anthropological figure begins to emerge. Some speak of transhumanism not as speculation but as a blueprint: a future in which language, symbols, and abstraction converge into a shared hypersensibility.

It is in this context that I introduce a concept of my own. I call it the *Sensorial Nexus*. The term is not drawn from existing posthuman or transhuman literature; it is proposed here to name a specific configuration that has not yet been adequately theorised.

By *Sensorial Nexus*, I mean a programmed sensitivity in which instinct is no longer refined through character, experience, or inner coherence, but shaped by algorithmic influences, ambient signals, and systemic feedback. In this configuration, individuals do not so much decide but rather synchronise. They do not deliberate but respond. The performative becomes spontaneous; the algorithm becomes that gut feeling taken as private. Reflexes are calibrated through likes, alerts, trends, and collective mood rather than through lived attunement to the world. Crucially, this does not appear as domination or coercion. The social mask is no longer worn, as it was in earlier forms of postmodern performance; it is absorbed. It melts into the skin, becoming inseparable from the subject and therefore harder to detect and harder to resist. What appears intuitive, emotive, or natural is, in fact, system-conditioned. The line between genuine intuition and automated reflex is blurred to the point of invisibility.

Bibliography

Ajana, B. (2013). *Governing through biometrics: The biopolitics of identity*. Palgrave Macmillan.

Alkhazaleh, M. S., Shloul, T. A., Shater, A., Almajali, H., & Mousa, J. (2025). Postmodern AI: A New Vision of Man's Relationship with Technology. *Studies in Media and Communication, 13*(2), 50. https://doi.org/10.11114/smc.v13i2.7435

Baudrillard, J. (1994). *Simulacra and simulation* (S. F. Glaser, Trans.). Univ. of Michigan Press.

Baudrillard, J. (2012). *The consumer society: Myths and structures* (Reprinted). SAGE.

Branda, F. (2025). Generated humans, lost judgment: Rethinking knowledge with AI. *AI & SOCIETY.* https://doi.org/10.1007/s00146-025-02748-2

Cowans, A. (2025). AI: A new paradigm of inference? *AI & SOCIETY.* https://doi.org/10.1007/s00146-025-02777-x

Dobrodum, O., Martyniuk, E., & Nykytchenko, O. (2024). Virtualization of culture and religion and artificial intelligence in the postmodern context of modernity. *SSRN Electronic Journal.* https://doi.org/10.2139/ssrn.4754801

Hamilton, I. (2011). Postmodernism and science and technology. In S. Sim (Ed.), *The Routledge companion to postmodernism* (3rd ed., pp. 94–108). Routledge.

Hooker, J. N. (1999). A postmodern critique of artificial intelligence. *47148 Bytes*. https://doi.org/10.1184/R1/6703226

Jameson, F. (2005). *Postmodernism, or, The cultural logic of late capitalism* (11. printing in paperback). Duke Univ. Press.

Lupton, D. (2016). *The quantified self: A sociology of self-tracking*. Polity.

Lyotard, J.-F. (2005). *The postmodern condition: A report on knowledge* (Repr). Manchester Univ. Press.

Marmolejo-Ramos, F., Workman, T., Walker, C., Lenihan, D., Moulds, S., Correa, J. C., Hanea, A. M., & Sonna, B. (2022). AI-powered narrative building for facilitating public participation and engagement. *Discover Artificial Intelligence, 2*(1), 7. https://doi.org/10.1007/s44163-022-00023-7

Melrose, S. (2011). Postmodernism and performance. In S. Sim (Ed.), *The Routledge companion to postmodernism* (3rd ed., pp. 194–204). Routledge.

Ross, P., & Maynard, K. (2021). Towards a 4th industrial revolution. *Intelligent Buildings International, 13*(3), 159–161. https://doi.org/10.1080/17508975.2021.1873625

Schwab, K. (2016, January 14). The Fourth Industrial Revolution: What it means and how to respond. *World Economic Forum*. Retrieved from https://www.weforum.org/stories/2016/01/the-fourth-industrial-revolution-what-it-means-and-how-to-respond/

Seth, J. (2024). *Public perception of AI: Sentiment and opportunity*. https://doi.org/10.48550/ARXIV.2407.15998.

Sontag, S. (2003). *Regarding the pain of others*. Hamish Hamilton.

Storey, J. (2011). Postmodernism and popular culture. In S. Sim (Ed.), *The Routledge companion to postmodernism* (3rd ed., pp. 204–215). Routledge.

Watson, N. (2011). Postmodernism and lifestyles. In S. Sim (Ed.), *The Routledge companion to postmodernism* (3rd ed., pp. 62–73). Routledge.

Yigitcanlar, T., Degirmenci, K., & Inkinen, T. (2024). Drivers behind the public perception of artificial intelligence: Insights from major Australian cities. *AI & SOCIETY, 39*(3), 833–853. https://doi.org/10.1007/s00146-022-01566-0

Chapter 3
Posthumans, Transhumans, and the Sensorial Nexus

The argument proposed so far is that postmodernity is not an abstract intellectual fashion, but a condition of experience that reshapes how meaning is perceived. The previous chapter traced how symbolic mediation, performativity, technological rationality, and media saturation progressively destabilised frameworks of sense-making, producing a condition in which representation circulates without reference and individuals are left navigating an excess of choice without reliable orientation. What I have done so far is nothing radical. The argument advanced stands within established traditions of thought. What I want to do now with this chapter is a shift in register. The analysis turns from established lines of interpretation to a more speculative and deliberately provocative mode of inquiry.

The dissonance I intend to highlight is structural. It is not a private feeling of confusion, but a mismatch built into the conditions of contemporary life. We are attempting, I argue, to navigate a world whose conditions have changed faster than the tools with which we interpret it. Reason, language, identity, tradition, and narrative coherence were shaped within modernity, a world where truth aspired to stability, categories retained authority, and the subject could be organised as a coherent project over time. Postmodernity disrupted those assumptions. Artificial Intelligence (AI) is now reworking that disruption. The result is not just confusion, but a mismatch between inherited forms of orientation and emerging modes of experience. We continue to rely on modern cognitive instruments—analysis, critique, fixed identities, rational explanation—to make sense of an environment increasingly defined by automation, predictive systems, and ambient computation. It is as if we are navigating a liquid terrain with conceptual tools designed for solid ground.

This chapter advances three deliberately bold and provocative claims.

First, we are no longer simply *within* postmodernity. We are moving beyond it, into its aftermath. Postmodernity has completed its work of dismantling foundations; what follows is a drift managed by external systems.

L. Loriga, *Instinct, Reason and the Self in the Aftermath of Postmodernity*, SpringerBriefs in Psychology, https://doi.org/10.1007/978-3-032-25339-2_3

Second, this drift gives rise to posthuman and transhuman imaginaries, where technological integration is no longer optional or aspirational but structurally entangled with how meaning, agency, and orientation are produced. When meaning, judgement, and orientation weaken, technological integration appears not as excess but as compensation. Systems begin to think, remember, predict, and decide where humans hesitate.

Third, what emerges from this conjunction of developments—postmodern fragmentation, symbolic saturation, and AI—is what I call the *Sensorial Nexus*. The term is deliberately evocative. It is meant as a way of naming the lived configuration that takes shape when symbolic mediation, technological infrastructure, and algorithmic prediction converge at the level of perception itself.

The aim here is neither to endorse a technological future nor to rehearse familiar dystopian clichés. It is to inquire into the anthropological stakes of what is already unfolding. In the aftermath of postmodernity, instinct—understood not as a fixed biological reflex but as an embodied, non-propositional mode of orientation, a pre-reflective openness toward the world prior to abstraction and deliberative reason, as suggested up to this point—does not disappear; it is reconfigured. What follows is complete automation: instinct as social reflex. What once emerged from bodily exposure to risk, uncertainty, and consequence is now increasingly outsourced to signals, metrics, and automated cues. Orientation is progressively shaped by systems rather than experience—filtered through likes, alerts, trends, predictive feeds, ambient moods, and collective noise. Instinct no longer arises from lived contact with the world, but from continuous modulation by external pre-programmed and carefully crafted signals.

This chapter therefore opens onto a fourth point: the question of resistance. As representation displaces experience and mediation precedes perception, the problem is no longer merely epistemic but existential. Under such conditions, resisting automation becomes necessary to avoid being reduced to a calculable variable within the system rather than an irreducible subject. What is required is a deliberate reclamation—a snatching back—of embodied, pre-reflective attunement from the colonisation of the *Sensorial Nexus*.

3.1 Beyond Postmodernity: The Aftermath of the Collapse

First things first: We are no longer within postmodernity. We are beyond it. We are living into its aftermath. Postmodernity completed its historical work by dismantling foundations, dissolving inherited narratives, and exposing meaning as contingent, symbolic, and reversible.

Its central operation was negation: the systematic unravelling of tradition, progress, and reason as organising myths. Yet negation presupposes something to negate. Although in the opening section of this chapter I claimed to propose three provocative claims, the idea that we left postmodernity behind is not new.

To call anything "obsolete," "finished," or "over" is clearly to fuse an allegation of previous existence with one of contemporary absence... (Kirby, 2009, p. 5)

Cultural periods end not because they evaporate, but because they cease to function as adequate ways of understanding the present. In this sense, postmodernism has not disappeared; it has exhausted its work of dismantling great narratives. That *incredulity toward metanarratives* (Lyotard, 2005, p. xxiv) is now *embedded as* 'common sense,' *as that which* 'goes without saying,' *within the digimodernist landscape* (Kirby, 2009, p. 6). What once operated as a critique now functions as a background. The challenge to authority, truth, and coherence no longer provokes reflection; it is assumed. The void left by the collapse of tradition and the consequent loss of orientation does not remain empty for long; it is increasingly stabilised by technical systems that do not resolve meaning but replace it with operation.

3.1.1 From Critique to Procedure

It would take something wrenchingly huge to sweep this away; I believe digital technology, essentially, is that something. (Kirby, 2009, p. 27)

What digital technology sweeps away is not tradition or foundations—those were already dismantled—but the very dominance of postmodernism as the organising critical framework. Digital systems do not repair the damage left by postmodern critique, nor do they restore shared meanings or authoritative narratives. Instead, they replace critique with procedure. They organise experience operationally, through platforms, interfaces, and automated processes, rather than through interpretation, deliberation, or truth claims. Orientation is no longer achieved by asking what something means or whether it is true, but by interacting with systems that assign relevance, visibility, and priority in advance. Culture, under these conditions, no longer orients itself through narrative, judgement, or belief. It orients itself through functionality.

3.1.2 Saturation, Cybertime, Cyberspace, and the Biological Limit

The idea that the future has disappeared is, of course, rather whimsical, as while I write these lines, the future is not stopping to unfold. But when I say "future" I am not referring to the direction of time. I am thinking, rather, of the psychological perception, which emerged in the cultural situation of progressive modernity... (Berardi, 2011, p. 13)

This belief is not marginal. There seems to be a pervasive acceleration of experience in everyday life. Speed is no longer externalised in machines or infrastructures, as it was under industrial capitalism and factory life, but internalised.

> *In the mechanical era the machine stood in front of the body, and changed human behaviour, enhancing their potency without changing their physical structure. The assembly line, for instance, although improving and increasing the productive power of labourers, did not modify their physical organism nor introduce mutations inside their cognitive ability. Now the machine is no more in front of the body but inside it. Bodies and minds therefore cannot express and relate anymore without the technical support of the bio machine.* (Berardi, 2011, p. 16)

The result is not merely faster circulation of signs, but a restructuring of lived experience itself. Once acceleration is internalised—once the machine no longer stands opposite the body but operates through it—the very relation between perception, meaning, and reality is altered. Experience is no longer mediated primarily through interpretation or reflective distance, but through immediate, technically formatted responsiveness.

> *Simulation is no longer that of a territory, a referential being, or a substance. It is the generation by models of a real without origin or reality: a hyperreal* (Baudrillard, 1994, p. 3)

Signs cease to point outward; they operate inwardly, producing effects without requiring interpretation. In its postmodern formulation, this condition remained largely semiotic and cultural. Simulation manifested as spectacle, parody, irony, and the play of surfaces. It still presupposed distance: the subject could recognise, decode, and even enjoy the instability of meaning. The argument proposed here now is that this distance has now collapsed.

Under contemporary conditions, simulation no longer unfolds primarily at the level of representation but at the level of perception, attention, and cognitive response. These conditions give rise to a form of capitalism organised around signs, affects, and cognitive performance rather than material production, one that '…makes affects, attitudes, attributes and ideas directly productive without materialising them – is the cellularisation of labour' (Berardi, 2011, p. 5). The consequence is temporal. Once production operates through semiotic flows rather than physical labour, its expansion is no longer constrained by material limits.

Digital networks, financial abstractions, and media infrastructures—what Berardi calls *cyberspace* (Berardi, 2011, p. 17)—can expand indefinitely. Signals circulate faster, platforms multiply, and informational demands intensify without encountering physical resistance. This expansion, however, encounters a limit elsewhere. It is a clash between cyberspace and cybertime, with this latter being '…the ability of social attention to process information in time' (Berardi, 2011, p. 17). While cyberspace designates the potentially infinite domain of digital circulation, cybertime names the subjective and biological time required to process it, which is necessarily organic. Unlike digital systems, attention and memory cannot be accelerated without cost. They are bound to the rhythms and thresholds of the nervous system. When the speed of semiotic production exceeds the organic capacity of cybertime, experience becomes saturated. The nervous system cannot keep pace with the density and velocity of stimuli. Meaning therefore does not collapse through critique, demystification, or ironic distance—as postmodern theory assumed—but through overload. Saturation replaces interpretation. Panic, desensitisation, and paralysis emerge not as psychological anomalies but as structural effects of a regime in which the expansion of cyberspace relentlessly outstrips the limits of cybertime. When attention, memory, and affect are mobilised beyond their physiological thresholds, exhaustion becomes structural rather than exceptional.

At this point, the clash between cyberspace and cybertime ceases to be merely cultural and becomes internalised. Power no longer confronts the subject as an external force; it operates through continuous responsiveness, self-monitoring, and optimisation. Control is not enforced against the body but enacted through it. What follows is not resistance through critique, but adaptation through adjustment—where technological integration appears less as domination than as relief and compensation for exhausted cognitive and affective capacities.

3.2 From Saturation to Dependency: The Transhuman Turn

It is time to address the second claim I intend to defend: that technological integration is no longer aspirational but is becoming increasingly a necessity. If postmodernity completed its work of destabilisation by exposing the contingency of narratives, identities, and truth claims, and we are now in its aftermath, what comes next, I propose, is not liberation or interpretive freedom, but dependency.

As cyberspace expands, the need to keep up with its infinite possibilities becomes a necessity, and cybertime must be stretched beyond its biological limits. One possible entry point into this tempting idea is the observation of an alleged shift in dominant forms of disorder, which can be read as diagnostic of broader social conditions: depression, attention fragmentation, burnout, and exhaustion appear to displace earlier pathologies structured around repression or prohibition. Overload is no longer experienced as an external assault but as an internal collapse—too much information to process, too many options to evaluate, too much visibility to sustain, and too little interruption for attention and desire to settle.

> *[Contemporary pathology is characterised] ...neither by bacteria nor by viruses, but by neurons. Neurological illnesses such as depression, attention deficit hyperactivity disorder (ADHD), borderline personality disorder (BPD), and burnout syndrome mark the landscape of pathology at the beginning of the twenty-first century. They are not infections, but infarctions; they do not follow from the negativity of what is immunologically foreign, but from an excess of positivity.* (Han, 2015, p. 1)

If infections name an immunological model of harm organised around an invading Other—enemy/foreignness—infarctions name breakdown as an implosion; an internal exhaustion produced by surplus positivity rather than external attack. They map a transformation in the grammar of power from negativity (prohibition, repression, boundary-making) to positivity (activation, optimisation, exposure, productivity).

In such a saturated environment, the subject does not so much defend itself against an enemy as burn through its own capacities, because the prevailing pressure is positive (more activity, more connectivity, more output) rather than negative (limits, refusals, boundaries). It is a type of violence *immanent in the system itself* or *neuronal violence* (Han, 2015, p. 6). Unlike immunological harm—attack/defence against an enemy—neuronal violence lacks negativity and works by saturation and overheating. Accordingly, what overwhelms is not primarily a prohibitive *No* from outside, but an internally lived compulsion to remain capable, visible, and productive. The dominant injunction no longer takes the form of *You must not*, but of *You can*, such that pressure is experienced as self-pressure and failure is lived as personal inadequacy.

3.2.1 Self-Exploitation, Visibility, and the Digital Panopticon

> *The violence of positivity does not deprive, it saturates; it does not exclude, it exhausts. That is why it proves inaccessible to unmediated perception.* (Han, 2015, p. 7)

Overload is often misrecognised as freedom or opportunity: positivity harms by more—more connection, more visibility, more outputs—so the subject cannot easily locate the source of coercion in an external authority. In such conditions, technology comes to seem less like liberation and more like a set of coping devices—filters, feeds, metrics, reminders, productivity systems—designed to render chronic saturation manageable. This shift corresponds to the displacement of disciplinary society—structured around prohibitions such as *May Not* and *Should Not*—by achievement society, whose modal verb is *Unlimited Can*, so that 'Prohibitions, commandments, and the law are replaced by projects, initiatives, and motivation' (Han, 2015, p. 9). This is why the achievement-subject tends toward auto-exploitation rather than resistance: domination is reconfigured as self-management, and breakdown appears as self-directed exhaustion instead of conflict with a clearly external adversary.

> *Today's achievement-subject deems itself free when in fact it is bound like Prometheus. The eagle that consumes an ever-regrowing liver can be interpreted as the subject's alter ego. Viewed in this way, the relation between Prometheus and the eagle represents a relation of self-exploitation. Pain of the liver, an organ that cannot actually experience pain, is said to be tiredness. Prometheus, the subject of self-exploitation, has been seized by overwhelming fatigue.* (Han, 2015, p. 35)

The tormentor is no longer best pictured as an external sovereign punishing the body, but as the subject's own alter ego that continuously consumes its capacities. In other words, *Promethean freedom* (Han, 2015, p. 35) is the form taken by internalised constraint under achievement conditions: the subject becomes both actor and target of performance violence, compelled to burn itself as fuel for its own projects.

A tempting parallel can be made with the Panopticon—Bentham's architectural model (Bentham, 2017) in which subjects are arranged in cells around a central watchtower so that they are fully visible while the observer remains unverifiable—thereby inducing self-regulation under the possibility of constant observation. The mental gymnastics required for such a leap from Promethean freedom to the Panopticon is that if in disciplinary power, the subject internalises the gaze to obey; in achievement society, the subject internalises the gaze to outperform—turning evaluation into self-optimisation rather than mere compliance.

> *Hence the major effect of the Panopticon: to induce in the inmate a state of conscious and permanent visibility that assures the automatic functioning of power. So to arrange things that the surveillance is permanent in its effects, even if it is discontinuous in its action; that the perfection of power should tend to render its actual exercise unnecessary; that this architectural apparatus should be a machine for creating and sustaining a power relation independent of the person who exercises it; in short, that the inmates should be caught up in a power situation of which they are themselves the bearers.* (Foucault, 1995, p. 201)

In Foucault's account, the Panopticon produces *a state of conscious and permanent visibility* through which power functions automatically. Read alongside what has been argued so far, that logic persists but is refunctionalised so that visibility is not only a mechanism of conformity but a performance imperative that intensifies self-monitoring and self-exploitation. What makes this linkage especially interesting in cyberspace (that distributed digital environment of platforms and interfaces) is that panoptic visibility no longer depends on a bounded architectural space—prison, school, factory—but is diffused through interfaces that convert conduct into continuous signals: dashboards, follower counts, streaks, read-receipts, responsiveness indicators, ratings, rankings, and *engagement* metrics. These are *practical* mechanisms by which subjects learn to act as if they are always on display—curating outputs, optimising availability, and tracking performance against imagined audiences.

3.2.2 From External Support to Cognitive Dependency

> *New media and communications technology are also diluting being-for-otherness... The virtual world is poor in alterity and the resistance it displays* and *...in virtual spaces, the ego can practically move independent of the "reality principle, which would provide a principle of alterity and resistance...* and finally *...increasingly, virtualisation and digitalisation are making the real disappear, which makes itself known above all through its resistance.* (Han, 2015, p. 42)

Digital systems do not only *watch*; they also reorganise the conditions under which attention, judgement, and refusal (negativity) can take shape—conditions increasingly *poor in interruption*, lacking *between-times*, with acceleration abolishing intervals (Han, 2015, p. 22). This distinction clarifies what is distinctive about contemporary visibility. *Cyberspace* tends to designate the networked territories or environments of digital interaction, while *cybertime* foregrounds the temporality those environments impose—always-on rhythms, real-time feeds, compressed response windows, and the expectation of immediate reaction. What are the consequences of all of this? One consequence might be that cognition—understood here as the processes of thinking, perceiving, remembering, and reasoning—should not be assumed to stop at the individual's biological boundary. The *hegemony of skin and skull* might indeed be now something to be argued for not something that can simply be assumed (Clark & Chalmers, 1998, p. 18). On this view, what matters is whether environmental elements are actively integrated into ongoing cognition. External resources might not merely be background conditions.

> *...the human organism is linked with an external entity in a two-way interaction, creating a coupled system that can be seen as a cognitive system in its own right. All the components in the system play an active causal role, and they jointly govern behaviour in the same sort of way that cognition usually does. If we remove the external component the system's behavioural competence will drop, just as it would if we removed part of its brain.* (Clark & Chalmers, 1998, pp. 8–9)

Think of your friend Otto, for example, who wants to visit, let us say, the Museum of Modern Art. One might argue that he—and most of us—does not try to remember the address in his head. Rather, the first thing he does is pull out his small notebook. He flips to the address page, finds the entry for the museum, and reads the address. Then he starts walking, checking the notebook again at a corner to confirm he is still heading the right way. If he is uncertain, he consults it again—like someone else might consult their biological memory without thinking about it. In that situation, the notebook is not just a passive reference sitting nearby. It is part of the ongoing loop that produces the successful behaviour: Otto's goal triggers looking; looking yields information; the information steers his next step; the next step triggers another check. Otto and the notebook are doing the work together in a coordinated, back-and-forth way. That is the kind of case that is described as a *coupled system* in the snippet above. What happens, however, if one takes away Otto's notebook? Maybe his ability to get to the museum drops in the same sort of way it would if you took away a relevant internal resource—because the notebook was functioning as a working part of the system that governed his behaviour.

A potential objection to this extended view of cognition is that cognition must be portable—something like a constant internal core that remains available across contexts. A sort of 'Naked Mind: a package of resources and operations we can always bring to bear on a cognitive task, regardless of the local environment' (Clark & Chalmers, 1998, p. 10). The worry is easiest to see in practical terms. Imagine two travellers dropped into an unfamiliar city and told to reach a specific address. One can form and retain a mental route, recognise landmarks, and recover from wrong turns using memory and internal orientation alone. The other reaches the destination only because there happens to be a street map at every corner—or because a device continuously supplies turn-by-turn guidance. If those external supports are removed, the second traveller's competence collapses. From the *Naked Mind* perspective, that fragility is precisely the point: if an ability disappears the moment the artefact or setting disappears, this is taken as evidence that the artefact is an *add-on* rather than a constituent of genuine cognitive capacity. In other words, what counts as cognition proper must belong to the portable inner kit, not to whatever scaffolding the environment contingently provides.

A possible rebuttal shifts the emphasis from strict portability to reliable integration. The question is not whether an external resource can be taken away in principle, but whether it is stably and automatically available in practice—so that it functions as part of the agent's standing cognitive repertoire. When the coupling is reliable, an external resource can count as part of the 'basic package of cognitive resources that I bring to bear on the everyday world' (Clark & Chalmers, 1998, p. 11). One might even go as far as to argue that human cognition is well adapted to exploit such dependable scaffolds: evolution *favoured* capacities aimed at *parasitising the local* environment in order to reduce memory load and transform the nature of problems.

> *...it may be that the biological brain has in fact evolved and matured in ways which factor in the reliable presence of a manipulable external environment. It certainly seems that evolution has favoured on-board capacities which are especially geared to parasitising the local environment so as to reduce memory load, and even to transform the nature of the computational problems themselves.* (Clark & Chalmers, 1998, p. 11)

Many of the resources that once looked like optional, contingent *add-ons* are now routinely carried, instantly accessible, and woven into action in real time. One might go so far as to argue that the reliance on external supports is not an occasional convenience but a default mode of cognitive functioning: we navigate, remember, recognise, and decide through stable loops that run across the brain–body–device–world. If anything, the last two decades have made the dependence that worried the *Naked Mind* intuition more visible and more pervasive, not less—because the external components are now designed to be continuously available and frictionless to consult (e.g. turn-by-turn navigation, camera-based recognition, always-on search), so that removing them can produce an immediate drop in competence in exactly the way the coupled-systems picture predicts.

Think of Google Maps. For many it is not an occasional tool but rather a continuously available guide that shapes orientation and action step by step. Remove it, and the drop in navigational competence can be immediate and substantial—not because the person has *lost* some optional extra, but because a routinely integrated part of their way of navigating has been disrupted. Google Lens acts on the same premises: instead of relying on internal identification and recall, the user recruits a stable perception–device–world loop to classify, retrieve, and decide in real time. Think now how old people used to remember phone numbers. A generation ago, it was normal to carry dozens of numbers in biological memory: home, work, relatives, neighbours, local services. People rehearsed them, dialled them repeatedly, and the repetition itself strengthened recall. If someone changed their number, you had to update your memory or your paper address book, and a forgotten digit was a genuine cognitive failure. Now the task has been reorganised. It is now reasonable to claim that few people can recite the numbers of even close family members, not because memory has suddenly weakened, but because memory is no longer the primary storage medium. The number is stored as a contact entry, retrieved by searching a name, and an action is performed by tapping rather than recalling. In the same way, other forms of memory have shifted: photographs that once existed as a small set of printed images you might mentally catalogue are now captured in bulk and offloaded from camera rolls into cloud storage and searchable galleries. Instead of remembering an event by retaining a stable internal representation, we often remember *that a record exists* and how to retrieve it: *it is in my photos*, *it is in the shared album*, *it is in the cloud*, and so forth.

The broader point is that everyday remembering increasingly involves managing access paths rather than storing content: knowing which device, which application, which folder, which keyword, and which account will retrieve what you need. In other words, what counts as competent memory practice has shifted from internal recall to reliable retrieval within a stable person–device–infrastructure system, where the *memory* is partly a routine of interaction with external storage rather than a purely internal archive.

The issue is not whether cognition ever depends on the world—and let us skip debates on solipsism, the tradition that only one's own mind is certain (see Sober, 1995 for an overview), as well as its connections with quantum foundations (among others, Rovelli, 2024; Zaghi, 2024; Zwirn, 2024); this is not the point—but whether some world-involving processes are integrated tightly enough to be counted as parts of cognition itself. This shift from an internalist to an extended view of cognition has implications for the moral and social domains as well, including the idea '...that, in some cases, interfering with a person's environment can matter morally in ways analogous to interfering with their person' (Clark & Chalmers, 1998, p. 18). This means that if certain environmental resources function as parts of someone's thinking and remembering in the same way that neural processes ordinarily do, then disrupting those resources can count as disrupting the person's cognitive agency itself. Here, I am not merely making a descriptive point about human reliance on tools; rather, when an external resource is reliably integrated into someone's cognition, blocking access to it is not always like taking away a convenience, but can be closer—also in moral significance—to impairing a mental capacity.

A simple illustration is Otto's notebook case: if a notebook functions as a person's standing memory store, then stealing it or preventing access can be morally closer to damaging memory than to removing an optional accessory. In contemporary terms, if a smartphone contact list, calendar, navigation system, or assistive interface is woven into a person's everyday cognitive functioning, then arbitrary deprivation, coercive manipulation, or targeted sabotage of that resource can undermine autonomy, competence, and responsibility in ways that resemble direct interference with the person's cognitive life. This applies not only to tools like Google Maps, Google Lens, or language models as portable aids: the same logic applies when the external component—such as a cell phone—gets integrated *into* the person.

Think of implantable brain–computer interfaces, where the relevant cognitive and agential routines can be organised around a stable feedback loop between neural activity, signal decoding, and action in the world. Neuralink's high-channel implant platform is explicitly framed as a route toward scalable, high-bandwidth neural recording (Musk & Neuralink., 2019). Endovascular approaches such as Synchron's stentrode—a stent with built-in electrodes inserted through blood vessels and positioned near the brain to record neural activity without open surgery—pursue a similar aim through the vascular system. Preclinical work has demonstrated chronic cortical recording from a stent-electrode array placed via catheterisation

(Oxley et al., 2016) followed by first-in-human clinical translation in severe paralysis using a fully implanted endovascular BCI system (Mitchell et al., 2023). A parallel line of evidence comes from intracortical microelectrode arrays, including 96-channel implants used in prominent demonstrations of direct neural control of a robotic arm by people with tetraplegia (Hochberg et al., 2012). Deep brain stimulation is an established treatment for advanced Parkinson's disease, supported by randomised trial evidence (Deuschl et al., 2006), and the neuroethical literature has examined how stimulation can raise questions about autonomy, agency, and how benefit is evaluated beyond symptom relief (Zuk & Lázaro-Muñoz, 2021).

Now I do not want to offer these examples as a mere shopping list of currently available neurotechnologies. Rather, they are meant to illustrate a shared structural feature: in each case, the person's intentions and competences are realised through an integrated biological–technical system whose behavioural capacity drops in a predictable way when the external component is removed or disabled, mirroring the sort of dependence ordinarily associated with internal cognitive loss. If the relevant environmental or technical component is part of how a person thinks, acts, or perceives in ordinary life, then interfering with it is not straightforwardly analogous to removing property; it can amount to interfering with the person's agency in the sense anticipated by the extended cognition argument's emphasis on tightly integrated, behaviour-governing couplings. In these cases, the portability objection—that cognition must be an entirely self-contained *inner kit*—loses much of its force. The interface is not an occasional tool one happens to consult but is engineered to be continuously present and reliably available, precisely the kind of stable coupling that makes a world-involving process a plausible candidate for counting as part of cognition rather than a mere add-on.

3.2.3 The Transhuman Threshold

Tightly integrated interdependencies—stable couplings between human capacities and technical systems—are not a new theoretical invention but a recurring feature of human cognitive history. Drawing on the palaeoanthropologist André Leroi-Gourhan, Stiegler (1998) argues that the very distinction between the human interior and the technical exterior is a historical illusion. What he calls *technics* does not simply mean *technology*, but the entire system of tools, artefacts, and symbolic supports—writing, machines, instruments, technical procedures—through which human life maintains itself across time. Technics is the *milieu* in which human memory, language, and temporality come to exist. He follows Leroi-Gourhan's insight that hominisation—the evolutionary becoming-human, marked by upright posture and the freeing of the hand, where '…the hand will necessarily call for tools … [which] will necessarily call for the language of the face' (Stiegler, 1998, p. 145)—and exteriorisation, '…the process in which the appearance of the human is the appearance of the technical', specified as 'the appearance of language' (Stiegler, 1998, p. 141), are one and the same process: from the freeing of the hand to the emergence of language, every step of human evolution is tied to the externalisation of cognitive functions and skill into material supports.

> *Interior and exterior are consequently constituted in a movement that invents both one and the other: a moment in which they invent each other respectively, as if there were a technological maieutic of what is called humanity. The interior and the exterior are the same thing, the inside is the outside, since man (the interior) is essentially defined by the tool (the exterior).* (Stiegler, 1998, p. 142)

The claim here is that human and technical mediation are one and the same thing. Humanity is born through the coupling of organism and artefact, cortex and flint, gesture and tool.

> *Flint is the first reflective memory, the first mirror.* (Stiegler, 1998, p. 142)

The human is therefore a being whose cognition is exteriorised, whose continuity depends on artefacts that survive individual life.

The hand frees the face, the tool calls for language, and both co-develop with the cortex. Stiegler radicalises this biological insight into an ontological claim: the exteriorisation of function into matter—what he calls *epiphylogenesis* or 'the conservation, accumulation, and sedimentation of successive epigeneses, mutually articulated' (Stiegler, 1998, p. 140). In this light, the growing dependence on external devices is not a modern deviation but a continuation of the same process. The more advanced and integrated the systems become, the more human cognition and agency rely upon them.

What contemporary discourse calls *transhumanism* merely renders explicit what has been true all along: that the human is a technical species whose evolution proceeds by exteriorising its own capacities. Where earlier prostheses extended the body, transhuman systems—implants, neural interfaces, algorithmic cognition—extend the conditions of thought itself. The philosophical question is thus no longer whether technology modifies humanity, but how far the process of exteriorisation can go before the very distinction between human and technical is dissolved.

3.2.4 Enhancement as Dependency

All this can sound like a feverish dream, and yet lingering on transhumanist scenarios becomes increasingly difficult to avoid. The question is no longer solely whether enhancement is ethically permissible, but whether there comes a point at which integration is so deep, and reliance so routine, that withdrawal would constitute a serious impairment of agency. In bioethical discussions, *enhancement* is typically analysed not as therapy—restoring normal function—but as augmentation beyond what is standard for the species, a distinction that immediately raises questions about where *normal* ends and *better* begins (Bess, 2010; Savulescu & Bostrom, 2009). The point is not merely definitional: once *better* is set against *normal*, questions of authority and evaluation immediately surface—who sets the baseline, whose capacities count as deficient, and which forms of life become implicitly treated as in need of optimisation. Seen against the backdrop of saturation, however, enhancement also acquires a distinctly compensatory sense.

The appeal is not only to surpass the human but also to keep the human functional under conditions that exceed biological tolerances: faster filtration, more dependable recall, steadier attention, and more consistent decision-making. In that register, the transhumanist thought experiment—why cultivate slow and fallible capacities when cognitive *modules* might be installed, outsourced, or continuously supported—reads less like distant futurism and more like an emerging common sense (Bostrom, 2004; Bostrom & Sandberg, 2009). In light of the earlier diagnosis of overload and drift, the *module* is no longer only a speculative implant; it includes mundane, always-available cognitive supports that already restructure what competence looks like—and what failure feels like—in everyday life.

If technological scaffolding functions as a compensatory support for weakened orientation, judgement, and memory, then removing it may not be a mere inconvenience but may amount to disabling the person in practice: competence collapses because the relevant capacities are no longer realised within the individual alone, but across an integrated socio-technical system. Technology, in this register, appears less as optional augmentation and more as a promise of reliability, optimisation, and functional continuity under conditions in which unaided agency is increasingly fragile. In its contemporary articulation, transhumanism presents itself as committed to the use of science and technology to expand human capacities and to overcome what it treats as remediable limitations, such as ageing, cognitive shortcomings, and involuntary suffering (for an overview of what transhumanism is, see, e.g. Bostrom, 2005; More, 2013). What matters here is the movement's diagnosis: that ordinary human cognition is slow, biased, inconsistent, and vulnerable to fatigue and that these weaknesses can increasingly be treated as objects of technical intervention. At the same time, the horizon of transhumanism is increasingly entangled with the possibility that artificial systems might not only assist human cognition but rival or surpass it. This possibility complicates the enhancement narrative: the *next step* may be framed either as improving humans through technological integration or as entering an ecosystem in which nonhuman cognitive agents become consequential participants in social, economic, and epistemic life. At this point the posthuman critique becomes unavoidable, because it asks whether the human should remain the measure at all and whether agency, value, and responsibility can still be organised around a single privileged centre (Ferrando, 2020; Hayles, 1999). In this context, then, transhumanism does not interrupt the argument; it makes explicit what the preceding pages already imply. Once technological supports cease to look optional—once they become the ordinary condition for maintaining orientation—technological enhancement begins to appear as the next step in an already established dependence: the internalisation, optimisation, and redesign of the very capacities that have been increasingly offloaded.

This also marks a hinge in the chapter's overall trajectory: the question is no longer only how technologies support cognition, but how they recalibrate the basic conditions under which the world is encountered as salient, actionable, and meaningful. In this landscape, even the transhumanist declaration is both a wonderful dream and a dystopian nightmare.

> *We recognise that humanity faces serious risks, especially from the misuse of new technologies. There are possible realistic scenarios that lead to the loss of most, or even all, of what we hold valuable. Some of these scenarios are drastic, others are subtle. Although all progress is change, not all change is progress.* (Humanity+, 2009)

3.3 The *Sensorial Nexus*: Automation of Instinct

It is time now to address the last claim and introduce the concept of the *Sensorial Nexus* to the discussion, which represents the apex of what has been argued so far: the summit and end-line of my line of reasoning. In the aftermath of postmodern fragmentation and the saturation of symbolic environments—that is, the collapse of shared narratives and stable meanings, while images, signs, and symbols multiply so densely that experience is increasingly encountered through representations rather than anchored by them—what is at stake is the attenuation of subjectivity as an intrinsically private, irreducible, and unrepeatable centre of experience.

3.3.1 Attenuated Subjectivity under Algorithmic Conditions

I need to be careful here. I do not propose an autonomous, algorithm-free subject—some interior sovereignty untouched by social mediation, technological infrastructures, or cultural influence. That picture would be implausible, and in any case, it would force this chapter into the metaphysical stand-off between determinism and free will, which is not my purpose. My claim is more modest and more specific: within socially and technologically shaped conditions, there remains a first-person orientation that can generate responses not wholly reducible to the cues that solicit them—responses that exhibit practical originality (improvisation, deviation, initiative) and that support moral discernment (the capacity to evaluate, endorse, refuse, and justify one's conduct). This orientation is not mechanically exhausted by external processes of formation such as education and socialisation. Under conditions of symbolic saturation and algorithmic governance, however, the space in which that orientation can operate can be narrowed and flattened: the field of salience is increasingly pre-arranged, the range of likely replies is pre-shaped, and the interval required for reflective recalibration is compressed. The result is not the disappearance of subjectivity, but its attenuation: a drift toward a more reactive, externally timed mode of experience in which it becomes harder both to discern what is genuinely one's own within algorithmically pre-shaped inputs and to stabilise endorsement or refusal over time.

3.3.2 Subjective Experience and the Privacy of Access

My starting assumption is that subjectivity—namely, '*…certain types of experience, which we call subjective because we alone have access to them*' (Mead, 2015, p. 166)—is emergent and relational in its conditions of formation, yet remains experientially first-person: intrinsically *mine* in terms of access and immediacy. The Self is what is emergent and relational. I will borrow George Herbert Mead's reasoning here for my proposal:

> *There are other contents of this sort, such as memory images and the play of the imagination, which are accessible only to the individual. There is a common character that belongs to these types of objects which we generally identify with consciousness and this process which we call that of thinking, in that both are, at least in certain phases, accessible only to the individual.* (Mead, 2015, p. 166)

This is the ordinary criterion for the subjective: privacy of access, the *thereness* of felt or imagined contents, the fact that some experiential materials—images, moods, pain—are available only from the inside. This privacy does not by itself constitute a Self, namely, a structure of conduct in which the individual becomes an object to themselves, which is '…something which has a development; it is not initially there, at birth, but arises in the process of social experience and activity' (Mead, 2015, p. 135). The shared feature of privacy 'does not necessarily give them the same metaphysical status' and that 'the self has a sort of structure that arises in social conduct that is entirely distinguishable from this so-called subjective experience of these particular sets of objects to which the organism alone has access-the common character of privacy of access does not fuse them together' (Mead, 2015, pp. 166–167). This means that 'We cannot identify the self with what is commonly called consciousness, that is, with the private or subjective thereness of the characters of objects' (Mead, 2015, p. 169).

3.3.3 The Self as Social Organisation of Conduct

The distinction here is between subjectivity and the Self. S*ubjective* names a kind of content, while the *Self* names a kind of social organisation of conduct. This is where the distinction between subjective and reflective becomes necessary. On the one hand are contents accessible only to the individual—memory images, imagination, moods, pain; on the other is reflective consciousness, which is not merely private interiority but a socially formed capacity.

> *Then there is another use of "consciousness" with which we have been particularly occupied, denoting that which we term thinking or reflective intelligence, a use of consciousness which always has, implicitly at least, the reference to an "I" in it.* (Mead, 2015, p. 165)

Reflection is private in the limited sense that it can occur 'to which we alone have access' (Mead, 2015, p. 166). It is not however just another private content alongside moods, images, or sensations. Reflection is rather a socially formed capacity: the internalised ability of the individual to take perspectives, anticipate responses, and regulate conduct in a shared world.

It is not merely experience happening but rather it is experience oriented—experience in which I can address myself, evaluate myself, and revise what I am about to do. This is why privacy is not enough to define what matters. Subjectivity, on the other hand, names a class of contents marked by privacy of access, that is, *what is privately present to experience.*

A Self, by contrast, is not a content but an organisation—a structure of conduct that allows the organism to take these contents up, interpret them, and integrate them into a socially intelligible life. Private contents do not automatically amount to selfhood. The Self is the patterned capacity to locate private contents—this pain, this mood, this memory—within a field of roles, norms, responsibilities, and expected responses. There is an internalisation process at work here. The Self becomes possible when communicative interaction is carried into inner conduct.

> *The self to which we have been referring arises when the conversation of gestures is taken over into the conduct of the individual form.* (Mead, 2015, p. 167)

In other words, the Self emerges when the individual can run social interaction inside themselves—when they can anticipate how another would respond, respond to that anticipated response, and thereby make their own conduct answerable in advance. This internalised dialogue yields a standpoint from which one can appear to oneself not merely as a bundle of feelings, but as a participant among participants—someone who can be assessed, obligated, excused, corrected, or praised. For this reason, the Self is inherently social: it is made possible by taking the standpoint of others, including the generalised attitude of the community.

3.3.4 Reflection, Public Orientation, and the I/Me Distinction

Once the Self is understood as this internalised social organisation, the difference between *subjective* and *reflective* becomes clear. Subjective contents can remain private without becoming shareable in form. Reflection, even when private in access, is structured as potentially public in principle. A proof, for example, may begin as something accessible only to the thinker, but it is already oriented toward communicability—publishable, contestable, transferable—because it is composed in terms that can become common property. A memory image or mood can remain private without loss; a justification is private only provisionally, because it is formed within norms of intelligibility that already anticipate an audience.

This also clarifies the practical meaning of the *I/me* distinction. The *me* is the socially organised side of the Self: the internalised set of expectations, roles, and communal attitudes that define what counts as appropriate, possible, shameful, admirable. The *I* is the organism's response to that organisation.

> *The "I" is the response of the organism to the attitudes of the others; the "me" is the organised set of attitudes of others which one himself assumes. The attitudes of the others constitute the organised "me," and then one reacts toward that as an "I."* (Mead, 2015, p. 175)

The *me* gives stability and social legibility; the *I* introduces novelty, initiative, and refusal. The key point is that the *I* cannot be fully given in advance because 'what that response will be he does not know and nobody else knows' (Mead, 2015, p. 175). It becomes visible only after the act—often first as memory, when the agent realises what has just been done.

> *The "I" gives the sense of freedom, of initiative. The situation is there for us to act in a self-conscious fashion. We are aware of ourselves, and of what the situation is, but exactly how we will act never gets into experience until after the action takes place.* (Mead, 2015, pp. 177–178)

This is the groundwork for bounded agency. Agency here is not sovereignty or insulation from social formation; it is the situated capacity to take up the attitudes that constitute one's *me*, evaluate them, and respond—sometimes by conforming, sometimes by deviating, sometimes by pressing for revision. In Mead's terms, we are not simply bound by the community; we are engaged in a conversation in which the community's response can be affected by what we do and speak.

3.3.5 The Sensorial Nexus as Engineered Social Internalisation

This anatomy of bounded agency is what allows the *Sensorial Nexus* to be introduced as a contemporary transformation of the conditions under which selves and subjectivities are organised.

> *Mind is nothing but the importation of this external process into the conduct of the individual so as to meet the problems that arise.* (Mead, 2015, p. 188)

If inner conduct is formed by the internalisation of an ongoing social-symbolic process—then changes in the external process necessarily reconfigure the internal one. The contemporary social process is increasingly mediated by platforms, metrics, feeds, and algorithmic selection systems that saturate the environment with symbols, reorder salience, anticipate response, and continually present a generalised attitude back to the individual, often in score-based form. This is not simply a new layer of media in front of experience; it is a reorganisation of the very material from which the *me* is built and the *I* must respond. The stakes are not confined to belief or opinion. What is being reorganised is the field of what shows up as relevant, what calls out response, what becomes thinkable in advance, and what counts as the ambient sense of what others think. In Mead's terms, this is a transformation in the ecology of gestures and responses that can be internalised—hence a transformation in how reflective selfhood is scaffolded.

3.3.6 Pre-reflective Orientation and the Erosion of the Interval

Private contents are intrinsically mine, as argued above, yet they are not yet a Self, since '…the common character of privacy of access does not fuse them together' (Mead, 2015, p. 167). The question, then, is how far contemporary conditions alter the practical ability to keep that distinction intact. If selfhood indeed depends upon taking the attitudes of others—ultimately the attitude of a generalised other, the '…organised community or social group which gives to the individual his unity of self' (Mead, 2015, p. 154)—then platforms and predictive systems increasingly manufacture, quantify, and stream that *other* back to the individual as an ambient presence. The organising standpoint of the Self is thereby less anchored in face-to-face reciprocity or relatively stable institutions, and more in an engineered, continuously updated field of cues that also colours what is immediately felt. Subjectivity remains private in access, but it is less and less privately formed: it is increasingly encountered as an orchestrated atmosphere in which the space for the *I* to respond is already pre-shaped.

3.3.7 The Final Provocation: Algorithmic Penetration of Pre-reflective Orientation

Read through Mead, the provocation becomes intriguing: if the Self is built by internalising the attitudes of the generalised other—much like a basketball player (Mead, 2015, p. 211) who learns to anticipate teammates' movements, reading the game not through explicit instruction but through absorbed patterns of coordination, thereby carrying the team's organised responses into their own conduct—then it is fair to assume that the generalised other can be fine-tuned by contemporary technological infrastructures. Such contemporary technological infrastructures, as argued up to now, do not operate on solid ground but rather on the vacuum left by the postmodern collapse of grand metanarratives, which previously functioned as stabilising frameworks of meaning and orientation and now act as fertile conditions for algorithmic cueing. Under such conditions, it is legitimate to imagine that this generalised other, fine-tuned by such technological infrastructure, might be able not only to populate explicit judgements (the Me) but also to begin patterning a pre-reflective readiness—*pre-reflective, embodied orientation toward the world, through which perception is made possible not as a product of cognition, but as its condition* (Merleau-Ponty, 2002). Such pre-reflective readiness comprises those non-propositional modes of orientation (what has been proposed so far generally as instinct, used here as an umbrella term) that precede reflection and articulation (namely, reason). The issue at hand, therefore—to rephrase for absolute clarity, as I wish there to be no misunderstanding in what I am proposing—is not whether one can escape algorithmic conditioning altogether (the Sensorial Nexus, which has replaced those metanarrative traditions mentioned earlier), but whether, under contemporary conditions, technological infrastructures increasingly strengthen the generalised other to such an extent that it extends its reach even into the private sphere of subjectivity.

Read through Mead, this does not imply that subjectivity ceases to be private in access, but rather that the social material internalised and processed by the Self becomes denser, more pervasive, and more continuously present, rendering it less distinguishable as a reflective exercise and increasingly more internalised as an inherently private endeavour. The generalised other internalised by the Self is therefore no longer drawn primarily from face-to-face interaction or relatively stable institutions alone, rooted in traditional metanarratives, but now also from algorithmically curated social attitudes, continuously assembled and reinforced through cybertime (the finite biological capacity to process information) and cyberspace (the infinite digital domain of circulating signals and data). This algorithmic curation operates through what was earlier described as a regime of positivity: a social logic in which pressure is exerted not through prohibition or exclusion, but through constant activation, visibility, responsiveness, and performance. The subject internalises a post-panoptic logic in which visibility is no longer imposed by a central authority but becomes a diffuse, ambient condition of participation, such that panoptic self-monitoring is fused with what was previously called Promethean freedom: self-optimisation and performance are experienced not as external coercion but as internally generated necessity, with the subject burning itself as fuel for its own projects.

In this sense, technological infrastructures do not merely mediate social influence; they compound and stabilise it, presenting an ambient and anticipatory social standpoint that is persistently internalised. What is encountered is not a single other, but an expanded, constantly updated field of expectations, evaluations, and probable responses that masks itself as one's own private sphere. This influence does not merely organise explicit judgements (the Me). Due to its pervasiveness and anticipatory character, it increasingly begins to shape the conditions under which response itself becomes possible (the I). The Self's internal conversation is thus entered into an already asymmetrically structured field, with fewer moments left unshaped by prior cueing. In other words, these internalised attitudes do not only structure reflective deliberation; they increasingly reach into pre-reflective readiness. At this level, what is shaped in advance is not belief, but salience itself: what appears, what calls for response, and what is silently filtered out before reflection begins.

The issue, therefore, is not whether conditioning can be avoided, but whether one can preserve or cultivate uniqueness—that is, whether attentional calibration and noise reduction (the capacity to regulate what one attends to and to limit saturation by competing signals) remain possible such that pre-reflective orientations are not wholly substituted by engineered cues. Framed in Mead's terms, the concern is whether the socially organised Me, increasingly trained by algorithmic environments, comes to dominate to such an extent that the space for the I—the organism's spontaneous, non-predictable response—is so compressed that it can no longer operate meaningfully.

The cultivation of uniqueness here is not sovereign self-construction. It is instead a realignment under technological and algorithmic pressure—an effort to preserve the interval in which originality can take hold, and in which the I, as the source of initiative and unanticipated response, can still interrupt, revise, or refuse what the Me presents. What is at stake is not the disappearance of subjectivity, which remains private in access, but the narrowing of the conditions under which its unrepeatable contribution can emerge.

Postmodern accounts kept symbolic instability at the level of representation and interpretation: meanings proliferate, irony and critique remain available as distances. Under contemporary conditions, as argued in the previous sections, mediation is increasingly installed at the level of perception and attention—before reflection gets traction. The question is no longer only what meanings are offered, but what becomes perceptually available as salient, how quickly it arrives, and how it arrives already affectively coloured. This is where Stiegler's diagnosis is especially useful: technics is not merely tools, but the exteriorisation of memory and temporality as conditions of subject formation (Stiegler, 1998).

Read alongside Mead, the implication is direct, and the urgency is clear. If the Self is the social organisation of conduct and subjectivity is the privacy of felt contents, then what we are currently experiencing in the present times is a condition in which the social organisation increasingly *enters* the felt contents themselves: private experience still belongs to myself alone, but it arrives already saturated with the attitudes, valuations, and timings of an engineered generalised other, so that subjectivity is experienced less as raw thereness and more as pre-shaped orientation. What is endangered is not freedom in the metaphysical sense, but the minimal space of first-person endorsement—bounded agency as the practical capacity to recalibrate one's attention, affect, and orientation.

3.4 Conclusion

We have reached the bottom of the barrel—scraped it thoroughly, perhaps in a way that risks sounding bleak. What this chapter has laid bare is not a hypothetical future but a present condition: a world in which the aftermath of postmodern fragmentation, digital saturation, and algorithmic anticipation have converged to reconfigure the most basic structures of experience.

At the centre of this analysis lies the *Sensorial Nexus*—the term I use to name the contemporary condition in which perception itself is mediated, modulated, and, increasingly, automated. This is not just about what we know or believe, but about how we *feel*, *attend*, and *respond*, even before reflection intervenes. In such a context, instinct—once understood as embodied openness to the world—is reprogrammed as reflex, tuned and guided by algorithmic rhythms and predictive cues. Under these conditions, subjectivity does not vanish but becomes increasingly preformed: a matter not of freedom, but of pre-arranged response.

To arrive at this diagnosis, the chapter unfolded in three interlocking movements. First, it argued that we are no longer within postmodernity, but in its *aftermath*—a historical condition in which there is little left for postmodern critique to dismantle, and in which inherited fragmentation no longer provokes reflection but simply persists. Second, it explored how this drift leads to *transhuman dependency*, where technological integration ceases to be aspirational and becomes compensatory: a means of sustaining cognitive and perceptual functions under saturated conditions. Third, it introduced the *Sensorial Nexus* as the point where these dynamics converge: a lived field in which symbolic mediation, technological infrastructure, and algorithmic governance shape perception itself—training instinct, modulating attention, and narrowing the scope for first-person deviation or reflection. This is, in a sense, the lowest point: not in tone, but in structure.

We have descended to the level where the very conditions of experience are being reorganised—where mediation does not simply frame what is seen, but governs how it is seen, felt, and acted upon. We scraped the bottom not to despair, but to understand. And now, it is time to rise again out of the midst and depths of this gloomy diagnosis. What follows is a parallel path—not a rejection of technology, nor a retreat into idealised authenticity, but a deliberate reorientation: one that gives priority to *instinct* over predictive cueing, to *attentional calibration* over algorithmic saturation. It is here that we begin our ascent—not into transcendence, but toward a new sensibility that can resist being fully formatted by the infrastructures it inhabits.

The next chapter therefore opens a different kind of inquiry: not into the collapse of symbolic organisation, but into the *possibility of recovery*—a cultivated instinct that preserves a space for originality, refusal, and attuned responsiveness within the very systems that threaten to automate them. This is where the question of resistance becomes practical: how can instinct become not only preserved, but practiced—as a mode of living perceptually, ethically, and socially in a world where even perception is no longer fully one's own?

Bibliography

Baudrillard, J. (1994). *Simulacra and simulation* (S. F. Glaser, Trans.). Univ. of Michigan Press.

Bentham, J. (2017). *Panopticon or the inspection house*. Anodos Books.

Berardi, F. (2011). *After the future* (G. Genosko & N. Thoburn, Eds). AK Press.

Bess, M. (2010). Enhanced humans versus "normal people": Elusive definitions. *The Journal of Medicine and Philosophy: A Forum for Bioethics and Philosophy of Medicine, 35*(6), 641–655. https://doi.org/10.1093/jmp/jhq053

Bostrom, N. (2004). The future of human evolution. In C. Tandy (Ed.), *Death and anti-death: Two hundred years after Kant, fifty years after Turing* (pp. 339–371). Ria University Press. Retrieved from https://nickbostrom.com/fut/evolution.pdf.

Bostrom, N. (2005). A history of transhumanist thought. *Journal of Evolution and Technology, 14*(1), 1–25.

Bostrom, N., & Sandberg, A. (2009). Cognitive enhancement: Methods, ethics, regulatory challenges. *Science and Engineering Ethics, 15*(3), 311–341. https://doi.org/10.1007/s11948-009-9142-5

Clark, A., & Chalmers, D. (1998). The extended mind. *Analysis, 58*(1), 7–19.

Deuschl, G., Schade-Brittinger, C., Krack, P., Volkmann, J., Schäfer, H., Bötzel, K., Daniels, C., Deutschländer, A., Dillmann, U., Eisner, W., Gruber, D., Hamel, W., Herzog, J., Hilker, R., Klebe, S., Kloß, M., Koy, J., Krause, M., Kupsch, A., et al. (2006). A randomized trial of deep-brain stimulation for Parkinson's disease. *New England Journal of Medicine, 355*(9), 896–908. https://doi.org/10.1056/NEJMoa060281

Ferrando, F. (2020). *Philosophical posthumanism* (Paperback edition). Bloomsbury Academic.

Foucault, M. (1995). *Discipline and punish: The birth of the prison* (A. Sheridan, Trans.; Second Vintage Books edition). Vintage Books, a division of Random House, Inc.

Han, B.-C. (2015). *The burnout society* (E. Butler, Trans.). Stanford Briefs, an imprint of Stanford University Press.

Hayles, N. K. (1999). *How we became posthuman: Virtual bodies in cybernetics, literature, and informatics*. University of Chicago Press.

Hochberg, L. R., Bacher, D., Jarosiewicz, B., Masse, N. Y., Simeral, J. D., Vogel, J., Haddadin, S., Liu, J., Cash, S. S., van der Smagt, P., & Donoghue, J. P. (2012). Reach and grasp by people with tetraplegia using a neurally controlled robotic arm. *Nature, 485*(7398), 372–375. https://doi.org/10.1038/nature11076

Humanity+. (2009). *The transhumanist declaration*. Retrieved from https://www.humanityplus.org/the-transhumanist-declaration.

Kirby, A. (2009). Digimodernism: How new technologies dismantle the postmodern and reconfigure our culture. *Continuum.*

Lyotard, J.-F. (2005). *The postmodern condition: A report on knowledge (Repr)*. Manchester Univ. Press.

Mead, G. H. (with Huebner, D. R., & Joas, H.). (2015). *Mind, self, and society* (C. W. Morris, Ed.; The definitive edition). University of Chicago press.

Merleau-Ponty, M. (2002). The spatiality of one's own body and motility. In *Phenomenology of perception* (pp. 112–171). Routledge.

Mitchell, P., Lee, S. C. M., Yoo, P. E., Morokoff, A., Sharma, R. P., Williams, D. L., MacIsaac, C., Howard, M. E., Irving, L., Vrljic, I., Williams, C., Bush, S., Balabanski, A. H., Drummond, K. J., Desmond, P., Weber, D., Denison, T., Mathers, S., O'Brien, T. J., et al. (2023). Assessment of safety of a fully implanted endovascular brain-computer interface for severe paralysis in 4 patients: The stentrode with thought-controlled digital switch (SWITCH) study. *JAMA Neurology, 80*(3), 270–278. https://doi.org/10.1001/jamaneurol.2022.4847

More, M. (2013). The philosophy of transhumanism. In M. More & N. Vita-More (Eds.), *The transhumanist reader* (1st ed., pp. 3–17). Wiley. https://doi.org/10.1002/9781118555927.ch1

Musk, E., & Neuralink. (2019). An integrated brain-machine interface platform with thousands of channels. *Journal of Medical Internet Research, 21*(10), e16194. https://doi.org/10.2196/16194

Oxley, T. J., Opie, N. L., John, S. E., Rind, G. S., Ronayne, S. M., Wheeler, T. L., Judy, J. W., McDonald, A. J., Dornom, A., Lovell, T. J. H., Steward, C., Garrett, D. J., Moffat, B. A., Lui, E. H., Yassi, N., Campbell, B. C. V., Wong, Y. T., Fox, K. E., Nurse, E. S., et al. (2016). Minimally invasive endovascular stent-electrode array for high-fidelity, chronic recordings of cortical neural activity. *Nature Biotechnology, 34*(3), 320–327. https://doi.org/10.1038/nbt.3428

Rovelli, C. (2024). Can Alice do science and have friends, in a relational quantum world? Solipsism and Relational Quantum Mechanics (Version 2). *arXiv*. https://doi.org/10.48550/ARXIV.2410.20012.

Savulescu, J., & Bostrom, N. (Eds.). (2009). *Human Enhancement*. Oxford University Press. https://doi.org/10.1093/oso/9780199299720.001.0001

Sober, E. (1995). Why not solipsism? *Philosophy and Phenomenological Research, 55*(3), 547–566. https://doi.org/10.2307/2108438

Stiegler, B. (1998). *The fault of Epimetheus*. Stanford Univ. Press.

Zaghi, A. E. (2024). Relational quantum dynamics (RQD): An informational ontology (version 2). *arXiv*. https://doi.org/10.48550/ARXIV.2412.05979.

Zuk, P., & Lázaro-Muñoz, G. (2021). DBS and autonomy: Clarifying the role of theoretical neuroethics. *Neuroethics, 14*(1), 83–93. https://doi.org/10.1007/s12152-019-09417-4

Zwirn, H. (2024). Convivial solipsism as a maximally perspectival interpretation. *Foundations of Physics, 54*(3), 39. https://doi.org/10.1007/s10701-024-00773-7

Chapter 4
Beyond Rationalism: Intuition, Habit, and Tacit Orientation

The previous chapter closed by arguing that, in the aftermath of postmodernity, instinct—understood up to this point not as a fixed biological mechanism but rather as a pre-reflective, embodied openness and orientation toward the world, a mode of attunement that precedes abstraction and deliberative reason, or '...our means or manner of opening on to a world we are already "in" or "of"' *(l'en être)* (Cataldi, 2008, p. 163)—has not vanished, but has instead been overwritten. It has been compressed into reflexes and synchronised with external cues that operate at the level of perception itself. Reason, by contrast, was presented as a propositional mode of orientation, an extension of that same embodied responsiveness into reflection and articulation. Instinct is reason's forgotten twin: an embodied orientation buried beneath layers of abstraction. The question, then, is how—given that reason can no longer reliably orient us—in the aftermath of postmodernity and under the emerging conditions of the *Sensorial Nexus*, instinct might still guide us before algorithmic absorption is complete, that is, before externally mediated forms of the Self fully pre-structure the conditions under which subjectivity is encountered (to borrow Mead's terminology).

The task of the present chapter is to propose forms of knowing and orientation that can preserve originality and make judgement possible where deliberative reason alone can no longer reliably arrive in time. To this end, I draw on three authors: Henri Bergson, David Hume, and Michael Polanyi. This analysis is not intended to eviscerate their respective bodies of work in details, but to extract a shared insight into pre-reflective modes of orientation that run through their thinking. By identifying the epistemic role of such orientations, the chapter prepares the ground for what follows: the question of how these modes of knowing might be cleared and rediscovered before it is too late—before the algorithmic architectures of the *Sensorial Nexus* fully pre-structure individuality through externally mediated patterns of attention, response, and lived experience.

L. Loriga, *Instinct, Reason and the Self in the Aftermath of Postmodernity*, SpringerBriefs in Psychology, https://doi.org/10.1007/978-3-032-25339-2_4

4.1 Instinct and Knowledge

A major strand of modern Western epistemology begins from the assumption that knowledge is primarily conceptual: the mind represents, classifies, and judges (see, e.g. McDowell, 2003; Rorty, 1979).

> *And this brings us face to face with the fact that most empirically minded philosophers are strongly inclined to think that all classificatory consciousness, all knowledge that something is thus-and-so, or, in logicians' jargon, all subsumption of particulars under universals, involves learning, concept formation, even the use of symbols.* (Sellars, 1997, p. 20)

If judgement is understood in these terms—as the application of learned concepts yielding a settled thus-and-so—the problem today is not its philosophical legitimacy but its temporal viability. In environments engineered to accelerate salience and response, reasons proliferate faster than they can be integrated into a stable judgement. Under conditions of algorithmic curation—where attention is continuously channelled and affect rapidly recruited—deliberation risks arriving late, functioning as commentary on a direction already taken. The question, then, is not whether reason remains valuable, but what makes judgement possible when reasons multiply faster than they can settle. One answer suggested by the preceding chapters is that orientation can and must also depend upon a non-propositional mode of orientation—felt, temporal, and tacit—without which rationality risks collapsing into mere instrumentality.

4.2 Bergson: Intuition as a Method of Knowing

Henri Bergson can serve as a starting point for mapping this parallel epistemic direction, namely, the attempt to think forms of knowing that do not proceed by abstraction, representation, and symbolic reconstruction, but by coincidence with lived movement itself. Where the dominant rationalist trajectory privileges analysis, conceptual mediation, and retrospective ordering, this alternative orientation begins from duration, intuition, and the immediacy of becoming rather than from its decomposition into stable elements. The point of departure here is methodological. Philosophers, Bergson notes:

> *...in spite of their apparent divergencies, agree in distinguishing two profoundly different ways of knowing a thing. The first implies that we move round the object; the second that we enter into it. The first depends on the point of view at which we are placed and on the symbols by which we express ourselves. The second neither depends on a point of view nor relies on any symbol. The first kind of knowledge may be said to stop at the relative; the second, in those cases where it is possible, to attain the absolute.* (Bergson, 1913, p. 1)

Here *relative* does not mean merely subjective or unreliable. It names knowledge that remains mediated by perspective and translation—knowledge of the object as represented within a framework. *Absolute*, on the other hand, does not mean infallible certainty. It indicates a mode of access that aims at coincidence with the object's own movement: grasping it from within rather than reconstructing it from without. If, as argued previously, algorithmic environments increasingly reorganise attention and affect before reflective appraisal can stabilise a judgement, then deliberation arrives late—after salience has been engineered and responses pre-shaped. A possible question, then, is not whether conceptual reason remains valuable, but what makes judgement possible *in time*, under conditions where reasons proliferate faster than they can settle. *Intuition* might be an answer, understood in contrast to analysis, with this latter being the procedure that approaches things from the outside by breaking them into describable parts, translating them into concepts, and relating them to what is already familiar and comparable.

> *By intuition is meant the kind of intellectual sympathy by which one places oneself within an object in order to coincide with what is unique in it and consequently inexpressible.* (Bergson, 1913, p. 6)

Intuition, in this sense, is not a spontaneous hunch but a method: an effort to grasp a phenomenon from within its own movement rather than by translating it into external coordinates, comparisons, or conceptual elements. By contrast, analysis proceeds by reduction—breaking the object into what can be redescribed in terms already familiar and shareable, that is, what it has in common with other things. Bergson's claim is not that analysis is useless, but that it characteristically converts lived continuity into representational substitutes—symbols, viewpoints, and decomposed elements—thereby risking a loss of what is singular, temporal, and qualitative in the thing itself.

4.2.1 Intuition and the Limits of Analysis

The relevance of Bergson's distinction between analysis and intuition becomes clear once it is situated within the temporal conditions described in the previous sections. Algorithmic curation is, in fact, not simply informational overload but temporal distortion: attention and affect are channelled such that reflective appraisal is continually outpaced—think of cyberspace and cybertime (Berardi, 2011, p. 17). Furthermore, when the object of knowledge is a process rather than a thing—something that *becomes,* for example, the experience of listening to a melody, which is lived as a qualitative flow but reconstructed by reason as a sequence of discrete notes—reason proceeds by translating *becoming* into a series of distinct, analysable states. In doing so, it spatialises time: what is lived as continuity is reconstructed as juxtaposition. This is not an error—at least according to Bergson—but rather a limitation intrinsic to analytic reason, which proceeds through *symbols and points of view* and is *compelled to turn* around its object, so that *description, history and analysis leave me here in the relative* (Bergson, 1913, pp. 4–7). What this procedure misses is *duration*: not time conceived as a sequence of discrete, externalised instants, but time as lived, in which states interpenetrate, and the past endures within the present. Duration, therefore, is not a succession of isolated points but rather:

> *...a succession of qualitative changes, which melt into and permeate one another, without precise out lines, without any tendency to externalize themselves in relation to one another, without any affiliation with number.* (Bergson, 2001b, p. 104)

We grasp such temporality not by placing past and present *side by side*, as one does with things in space, but when they form *an organic whole*, such that '...we perceive them in one another ... the notes of a tune, melting, so to speak, into one another' (Bergson, 2001b, p. 101). Duration, then, is not composed of countable parts and bears no resemblance to the spatial medium in which we typically represent time. It is irreducible to spatial terms. Spatiality permits the measurement and comparison of fixed intervals, but duration cannot be divided without distortion. We commonly mistake time for space because of our habit of symbolically representing it.

> *Duration thus assumes the illusory form of a homogeneous medium, and the connecting link between these two terms, space and duration, is simultaneity, which might be defined as the intersection of time and space.* (Bergson, 2001b, p. 110)

This symbolic substitution is fit to capture the mathematical and scientific conception of time but fails to grasp the experience of lived becoming.

To comprehend such becoming requires not further conceptual analysis but a different mode of knowing, which Bergson names *intuition*—that *intellectual sympathy* referenced above. This is not the negation of reason but its limit-point: intuition does not discard reason but redirects it, toward an immediate apprehension of inner movement. For this reason, relative knowledge, rooted in spatialisation and symbolisation, remains incapable of seizing true becoming. In everyday experience, we are often unaware of how consciousness naturally distorts duration. For example, when several strokes of a clock are heard inattentively, they are not initially counted as discrete units. Yet, when we turn our attention back, we find we can recall them—not as a numerical sum, but as a qualitative whole, like a phrase of music. The successive sounds have melted into one another, forming a unity whose rhythm can be retrospectively analysed, but which was first apprehended as a single, indivisible quality. It is only when we attempt to count the strokes that we isolate them, placing them side by side like points in space. In such cases, the number is perceived not as quantity, but as quality—duration as it is immediately lived. However, this original experience is typically replaced by a symbolical representation derived from space. Instead of the lived continuity of inner life, we come to know only its shadow—its externalised image, projected into a homogeneous medium.

> *Consciousness, goaded by an insatiable desire to separate, substitutes the symbol for the reality, or perceives the reality only through the symbol.* (Bergson, 2001b, p. 128)

This desire to separate leads us to fix our fluid, ever-changing impressions into stable objects, to translate the mobile into the immobile, and to confuse the becoming of the Self with the static forms imposed by language.

This use of *Self* should be distinguished from Mead's account: whereas Mead sees the Self as socially constructed through symbolic interaction, Bergson refers here to a more fundamental, pre-conceptual continuity of consciousness—what he elsewhere calls the *fundamental self* (Bergson, 2001a)—a pre-reflective, continuous flow of inner experience prior to its fragmentation through language and social life.

The outcome of this symbolic fixation is a false clarity—precise, but impersonal—in which inner experience is misrecognised in the very act of being expressed. What endures is no longer the Self in its living duration, but a fragmented image suited to social communication and abstract thought. For Bergson, this is precisely why another mode of knowing is required—one that does not break becoming into parts but grasps it from within.

What emerges is not a rejection of reason, but a clarification of its limits. Analytic thought proceeds by separation, symbolisation, and spatialisation; it renders experience intelligible by arresting its movement. Yet when the object of knowledge is *becoming* itself, this procedure necessarily distorts what it seeks to grasp. The alternative outlined here is a mode of knowing capable of coinciding with duration, preserving the qualitative continuity of experience rather than replacing it with static representations. Intuition therefore can be a disciplined method of knowing—one that remains answerable to lived temporality where symbolic reason can only arrive after the fact.

4.3 Hume: Passion, Habit, and the Limits of Reason

Bergson's critique concerns what analytic reason can know; Hume's concerns what reason can do. Where Bergson shows that analytic reason cannot grasp *becoming* as it is lived, David Hume shows that reason cannot initiate or sustain action without a prior, non-rationally generated orientation.

Reason alone cannot move the will: it can discover relations, correct errors, and organise means, but it does not generate ends or supply the impetus required for action to occur.

> *Nothing is more usual in philosophy, and even in common life, than to talk of the combat of passion and reason, to give the preference to reason, and to assert that men are only so far virtuous as they conform themselves to its dictates.* (Hume, 2003, p. 216)

The assumption here is that *virtue*—namely, that which merits moral approbation and regulates conduct—consists in deference to reason. The good agent is one who governs action by rational dictates, treating competing motives or passions as forces to be disciplined, overridden, or brought into conformity with a higher rational standard. Moral worth is thus identified with the successful subordination of inclination to rational judgement. This model presupposes not only that reason can determine what ought to be done but also that it can exercise temporal authority over motivation itself—that it can initiate, sustain, and direct action independently of the affective orientations from which willing ordinarily arises.

For Hume however, this perspective cannot be sustained. Rather than treating reason as a source of motivation or moral authority, reason operates within limits set by what moves the will. Reasoning, on its own, does not supply the motivating force required for willing and action and, therefore, cannot operate as an independent counterweight capable of overruling passion in directing the will.

4.3.1 The Scope of the Understanding

The argument that reason cannot initiate or sustain action rests on a distinction concerning what the understanding can do by its own operations, that is, the faculty responsible for reasoning, inference, and the comparison of ideas. Demonstrative reasoning, in Hume's sense, refers to reasoning concerned with relations of ideas, such as those found in mathematics and logic, where conclusions follow with necessity from their premises.

> *All reasonings may be divided into two kinds, namely demonstrative reasoning, or that concerning relations of ideas, and moral reasoning, or that concerning matter of fact and existence.* (Hume, 2007, p. 25)

Relations of ideas concern conceptual necessity, not action. Demonstrative reasoning therefore cannot originate motives, since its proper object lies in the comparison of ideas rather than in willing.

> *As it's proper province is the world of ideas, and as the will always places us in that of realities, demonstration and volition seem, upon that account, to be totally remov'd, from each other.* (Hume, 2003, p. 216)

The implication is not a rejection of reason or an epistemic scepticism about its value, but a principled restriction of its scope. Demonstrative reasoning remains indispensable for ordering thought, establishing relations of ideas, and correcting error. What it cannot do, on its own, is supply the motivational force that renders thought action-guiding or temporally effective, since willing requires an orientation toward reality that demonstrative reasoning, by its nature, does not provide.

The same limitation applies when the understanding moves from demonstration to probable reasoning about experience. Causal inference can inform action by revealing how events are connected, but it does not generate the orientation in virtue of which action is undertaken. It operates within a field of concern already structured by attraction and aversion—by passions, habits, and affective dispositions that render certain outcomes salient in the first place. Reason thus guides action only insofar as an orientation toward action already exists.

> *Reason is, and ought only to be the slave of the passions, and can never pretend to any other office than to serve and obey them.* (Hume, 2003, p. 217)

The point is not to licence caprice, but to specify the structure of agency. Deliberation can correct error and redirect strategy; it can revise beliefs about what exists and about which means will achieve a given end. But it cannot generate the ends in virtue of which correction and redirection matter. Reason therefore presupposes an orientation it cannot itself produce or formalise. To call an affection unreasonable does not mean that the passion itself is at fault, but that the judgement accompanying it is mistaken—either through a false supposition about the existence of its object or through an error concerning the means required to achieve it. Reason's authority is thus primarily corrective and instrumental, not legislative over ultimate ends or constitutive of value itself. This dependence of judgement upon pre-reflective orientation becomes more explicit in moral psychology.

4.3.2 Moral Salience and Affective Orientation

Moral distinctions—in other words, the differences by which actions, characters, or motives are experienced as worthy of approval or disapproval—if they are to guide conduct, cannot be grounded in a faculty that merely represents and compares, since moral appraisal is essentially action and attitude-shaping and therefore temporally situated within lived responsiveness. Take the case, for example, of the *wilful murder:*

> *Take any action allow'd to be vicious: Wilful murder, for instance. Examine it in all lights, and see if you can find that matter of fact, or real existence, which you call vice. In whichever way you take it, you find only certain passions, motives, volitions and thoughts. There is no other matter of fact in the case. The vice entirely escapes you, as long as you consider the object. You never can find it, till you turn your reflexion into your own breast, and find a sentiment of disapprobation, which arises in you, towards this action. Here is a matter of fact; but 'tis the object of feeling, not of reason.* (Hume, 2003, p. 244)

No matter how exhaustively one itemises an action's observable features or psychological components—that is, breaking the action down into everything that can be described from the outside, the vice, namely, the moral wrongness or blameworthiness of the action—is not encountered as a detachable property discoverable by inspection. So long as attention remains confined to the object—its describable elements, intentions, or outcomes—the moral quality eludes capture. It becomes salient only when reflection turns inward toward the observer's own response, and a sentiment of disapprobation arises as a reaction to the action so conceived.

Think again of a person being publicly humiliated—for example, by being shouted at in front of others, regardless of whether the action is ultimately judged right or wrong. One can list every observable feature of the act: the words spoken, their tone, the timing, the setting, the target's reaction, and even the speaker's stated intention. Yet none of these features, taken alone or together, contains the wrongness of the act as a property discoverable by inspection. That wrongness becomes salient only when the observer responds affectively—through discomfort, indignation, or disapproval—by which the action is apprehended as morally objectionable rather than as a neutral sequence of facts. Moral salience—that is, the way an action stands out as calling for approval or disapproval rather than remaining morally neutral—therefore, is not an optional judgement appended after neutral description. It is a mode of responsiveness without which the moral dimension does not come into view at all as morally significant. Moral judgement, like action, presupposes an affective orientation that reason can articulate but not originate.

4.3.3 Habit, Belief, and Moral Perception

Hume's wider moral psychology situates the affective responses through which actions acquire moral salience within shared human nature and social mediation—most notably through sympathy (see, e.g. his disambiguation of the origin of the natural virtues and vices) (Hume, 2003, pp. 293–301)—so that moral perception is cultivated, stabilised, and corrigible within forms of life rather than generated in isolation by individuals. The background enabling moral discrimination is not itself produced by syllogistic reasoning. It is a trained sensibility, one that can be educated, narrowed, distorted, or intensified through experience, practice, and social interaction. The same dependence on pre-reflective orientation extends beyond moral judgement to belief itself: belief, like action and moral appraisal, presupposes a pre-reflective orientation—that is, a habitual and affective attunement, that structures expectation prior to deliberation—which reason can organise and refine but does not itself generate. The transition from repeated experience to expectation cannot be grounded in demonstrative or probable reasoning alone. What carries the mind beyond present impressions is what Hume calls *habit or custom*: a learned disposition formed through repetition that enables anticipation and projection and which functions as the background condition of ordinary cognition:

> *All inferences from experience, therefore, are effects of custom, not of reasoning. Custom, then, is the great guide of human life.* (Hume, 2007, p. 32)

Custom is not presented as an unfortunate irrational residue, but as a necessary condition of practical intelligibility. Without it, experience would remain episodic and inert, incapable of sustaining projection, anticipation, or the adjustment of means to ends. Habit supplies the temporal continuity without which neither judgement nor action can stabilise. The same orientation governs belief. This latter, in fact, is not treated as a purely propositional assent added to an idea, but as a distinctive manner of conceiving—an experiential modification that gives certain representations practical force:

> *...the difference between fiction and belief lies in some sentiment or feeling, which is annexed to the latter, not to the former, and which depends not on the will, nor can be commanded at pleasure.* (Hume, 2007, p. 35)

Belief, on this account, is inseparable from salience—that is, from the way certain ideas stand out as authoritative rather than merely conceivable. What distinguishes belief from mere imagination is not logical form but felt authority: the way certain ideas acquire weight, steadiness, and influence over attention and action. Belief, like moral judgement and action, thus depends upon a habituated orientation that precedes reflective endorsement.

Across action, moral judgement, and belief, the analysis converges on a common limitation. Reason does not, by itself, generate the ends of action, the salience of moral distinctions, or the felt authority of belief. Its operations presuppose a field already shaped by habit, sentiment, and affective attunement. Within this field, reason can correct error, organise relations, and extend reflection, but it does not supply the conditions under which judgement first becomes possible. What allows reasons to matter in practice is a prior susceptibility through which certain possibilities, expectations, and responses come to stand out as significant.

4.4 Polanyi: Tacit Knowledge and Skill

The preceding sections introduced the ideas that neither judgement nor belief is generated by reason alone but presupposes a pre-reflective orientation that enables deliberation to function in time. Polanyi takes this claim one step further by relocating it within epistemology itself. If Bergson shows that analytic reason approaches its object indirectly through symbolic reconstruction, and if Hume shows that reason can neither generate ends nor secure belief without prior affective and habitual orientation, Polanyi argues that even explicit knowledge depends upon a tacit, embodied background that guides understanding in advance of articulation and cannot be fully rendered explicit without loss.

4.4.1 Tacit Knowledge and the Limits of Explicit Knowing

> *I shall reconsider human knowledge by starting from the fact that we can know more than we can tell.* (Polanyi, 2009b, p. 4)

What is proposed is not that knowledge is ineffable in principle, but that competent judgement routinely relies on subsidiary awareness—bodily skills, perceptual discriminations, and contextual cues that function as conditions of knowing without presenting themselves as explicit premises. Such reliance is not accidental but structurally necessary. Knowing has a characteristic directional form: in any act of knowing, attention is directed *from* these subsidiary elements *toward* a focal object or meaning, so that what supports understanding recedes from view as understanding itself comes into focus.

> *...in an act of tacit knowing we attend from something for attending to something else; namely, from the first term to the second term of the tacit relation.* (Polanyi, 2009b, p. 10)

And again

> *...we comprehend the entity by relying on our awareness of its particulars for attending to their joint meaning.* (Polanyi, 2009b, p. 13)

The particulars from which we attend—the *proximal term*, namely, the subsidiary elements that support understanding, such as bodily posture, sensorimotor coordination, perceptual cues, and contextual familiarity (see, e.g. the tacit knowing section in Polanyi, 2009a)—are not objects of focal awareness, yet they are actively integrated in the act of knowing. They function as the tacit background from which attention is directed toward a focal meaning. When attention is redirected toward these subsidiary elements themselves, the integration collapses rather than becoming more explicit. Tacit knowing therefore cannot be converted into a set of rules or premises without remainder.

Think for example, recognising a familiar face in a crowd. One does not attend focally to the individual features—the spacing of the eyes, the curve of the mouth, the texture of the skin—and then infer recognition by combining them. Rather, these particulars are relied upon subsidiarily, while attention is directed toward the face as a meaningful whole. If one attempts to focus explicitly on the individual features in order to reconstruct recognition step by step, the immediate sense of familiarity can weaken or disappear altogether. The knowing works only so long as the particulars remain tacitly integrated rather than made objects of focal scrutiny. This structure gives epistemic form to a dependence already traced in the preceding sections. What Bergson analyses as the limits of analytic reason in grasping duration—where understanding must coincide with lived movement rather than reconstruct it symbolically—and what Hume identifies in habit, custom, and affective orientation as the conditions enabling belief and action are here articulated as conditions of intelligibility within knowing itself.

Explicit reasons function only because a tacit background has already organised salience, relevance, and confidence. This is not a rejection of rationality, but an account of the conditions under which rational articulation and justification are possible at all. The modern ideal of complete transparency and detachment in knowledge—according to which all knowing should be fully explicit, formalised, and inspectable from the outside—proves internally unstable: attempts to eliminate tacit participation from knowing are not merely unrealistic but destructive. Knowledge does not fail because it contains tacit elements; it fails when those elements are forcibly brought under focal scrutiny.

> *We can see now how an unbridled lucidity can destroy our understanding of complex matters. Scrutinize closely the particulars of a comprehensive entity and their meaning is effaced, our conception of the entity is destroyed.* (Polanyi, 2009b, p. 18)

Excessive precision can undermine understanding rather than deepen it. When attention is driven toward the isolated particulars that support a complex entity, the coherence that renders it intelligible as a whole dissolves. Redirecting focus from focal meaning to subsidiary elements causes the integrative act of knowing to collapse, leaving behind discrete components stripped of the functional relations through which they originally made sense—much as isolating individual brushstrokes can obscure the unity of a painting rather than clarify it. The project of rendering all knowledge fully explicit undermines itself, because explicit articulation always presupposes a tacit background that cannot be eliminated without loss.

> *I think I can show that the process of formalizing all knowledge to the exclusion of any tacit knowing is self-defeating. For, in order that we may formalize the relations that constitute a comprehensive entity, for example, the relations that constitute a frog, this entity, i.e., the frog, must be first identified informally by tacit knowing; and, indeed, the meaning of a mathematical theory of the frog lies in its continued bearing on this still tacitly known frog.* (Polanyi, 2009b, pp. 20–21)

Articulated knowledge—that is, articulated rules, theories, or instructions that present knowledge as something that can be stated, codified, and consulted from the outside—can function as knowledge only insofar as they are interiorised and relied upon tacitly; they cannot replace the tacit integrations on which their use depends.

> *...the ideal of a comprehensive mathematical theory of experience which would eliminate all tacit knowing is proved to be self-contradictory and logically unsound.* (Polanyi, 2009b, p. 21)

4.4.2 Skill, Performance, and Destructive Analysis

Knowing is not a passive representation but as an embodied achievement sustained by skill. It is something one does rather than merely possesses, and it depends on a tacit organisation of particulars that cannot be replaced by explicit rules. Rules of art may guide practice, but they do so only insofar as they are absorbed into practical mastery; they do not determine performance from the outside. Skill operates through a background integration that remains effective only while it is not made the object of focal scrutiny.

Think of a pianistic performance, to borrow Polanyi's own example. Attempts to explain musical *touch* by reducing it to isolated physical variables can lead to the mistaken conclusion that no genuine difference exists between novice and virtuoso. Such conclusions arise from *destructive analysis* (Polanyi, 2012, pp. 52–54): an approach that seeks to explain skilful performance by decomposing it into isolated, measurable components, and in doing so explains away the very capacity it aims to understand. In the case of pianistic performance, this takes the form of analysing tone production purely in terms of the mechanics of key, hammer, and string. The sound produced by a piano key appears to be fully determined by the speed of the hammer at the moment it strikes the string. If this were sufficient, there would be no principled difference between the tone produced by a novice and that produced by a virtuoso, provided that the hammer velocity were the same. The point here is not that such physical analysis is false, but that it is incomplete. By restricting attention to a narrow set of variables, it overlooks how the pianist's bodily engagement with the instrument contributes to tone quality in ways that cannot be captured by those variables alone. Even when the speed imparted to the hammer remains constant, the depression of the key can generate different kinds of noise, which mingle with the sounded note and subtly modify its quality. These differences are perceptible to trained listeners and responsive to the pianist's touch, yet they disappear from view once performance is reduced to a schematic physical model.

The epistemic error here lies in mistaking what can be isolated and measured for what is sufficient to explain the skill. By dismantling the performance into discrete elements, destructive analysis dissolves the tacit integration through which those elements function together as a meaningful whole. When attention is redirected from the musical task to the bodily details of execution, this integrative organisation can break down, and performance may deteriorate accordingly:

> *If a pianist shifts his attention from the piece he is playing to the observation of what he is doing with his fingers while playing it, he gets confused and may have to stop.* (Polanyi, 2012, p. 58)

The limits of explicit articulation are not accidental shortcomings but structural features of knowing itself. Skill cannot be exhaustively specified without undermining the integrations that make it effective. What such analysis succeeds in isolating are relatively objective elements; what it dissolves is the tacit, purposive organisation through which those elements cohere as a meaningful whole. In this respect, the analysis converges with points already established earlier: judgement does not arise from reflective reasoning alone but depends upon a background orientation that precedes and sustains it. Knowing, like acting and valuing, is grounded in a pre-reflective organisation that cannot be replaced by further analysis without loss.

4.5 Conclusion

The task of this chapter has been to establish that the appeal to instinct is neither speculative nor nostalgic but grounded in a well-established line of philosophical and empirical reasoning that runs parallel to the predominance of deliberative rationality. By turning to Bergson, Hume, and Polanyi, I meant to address that orientation has always depended upon a pre-reflective, embodied orientation that reason presupposes rather than generates. What I refer to here, conventionally, as *instinct*—used as an umbrella term for non-propositional modes of orientation such as intuition, tacit knowing, or sensibility—is not an irrational residue within human cognition, but the condition under which orientation can occur at all, especially where time, uncertainty, and complexity preclude exhaustive deliberation.

Across these accounts, a consistent limitation of deliberative reason emerges. Analytic intellect cannot grasp becoming as it unfolds, but only reconstruct it retrospectively through spatialised symbols; coinciding with movement requires a different mode of access. Action, belief, and moral judgement likewise do not originate in reasoning alone, but presuppose a prior orientation supplied by habit and sentiment, within which reason intervenes only secondarily. Even explicit knowledge, finally, depends upon tacit, embodied discrimination that cannot be fully articulated without loss. In each case, the claim is not anti-rational but delimiting: reason remains indispensable, yet it operates within a field of salience and relevance that it does not itself produce. The idea of *destructive analysis* is especially instructive in this regard. The attempt to render knowledge fully explicit—by decomposing skill, judgement, or understanding into isolable components—does not merely risk incompleteness; it undermines the very integrations that make competent performance possible. What destructive analysis reveals are isolated, relatively objective facts; what it destroys is the personal, purposive organisation through which those facts function as a meaningful whole.

Under contemporary conditions, this insight acquires renewed urgency. Projects aimed at total codification—whether in Artificial Intelligence (AI) systems, large language models (LLM), algorithmic decision-making, or predictive governance—do not overcome this limitation but intensify it, scaling formal representation while displacing the tacit orientations through which judgement and responsibility are constituted. The risk is not only technical oversimplification, but anthropological distortion: the reconfiguration of human agency as something to be anticipated, managed, or replaced by externally generated representations rather than sustained through situated orientation. When tacit orientation is treated as noise to be eliminated rather than as the enabling background of judgement, the individual is displaced from the processes through which agency and responsibility take shape.

The *Sensorial Nexus* names a contemporary condition in which salience, relevance, and affective readiness are increasingly pre-arranged by external systems operating at the level of perception itself. Under such conditions, instinct does not disappear; it is overwritten. Embodied openness to the world is compressed into reflex and synchronised with algorithmic cues that anticipate response before judgement can stabilise. What is lost is not speed, but openness: the capacity for orientation to remain answerable to reality rather than merely responsive to prompts.

The degradation of instinct under conditions of saturation does not yield greater rationality. It produces hesitation, brittleness, and dependency. When orienting capacities are weakened, deliberation cannot compensate; instead, judgement becomes increasingly reliant on external systems that promise reliability by pre-empting decision altogether. Instinct, once the ground of situated judgement, risks being replaced by automated responsiveness—reaction without inward clearance. What has been named instinct, intuition, or tacit knowing is not an alien or irrational residue within judgement, but its enabling ground. Instinctive orientation enables action not because it bypasses reasoning, but because it makes reasoning possible within real-time constraints. It supplies the initial organisation of salience and relevance without which deliberation would remain inert or paralysed. Instinct, then, is neither a primitive impulse nor a romanticised faculty, but a cultivated, embodied capacity for situated orientation—one without which reason cannot function in time.

The task that follows is therefore explicit: to propose a possible way of purging this orienting capacity from the overwhelming and increasingly comprehensive effects of the *Sensorial Nexus*. This proposal takes the form of the *DIEM Method*, a framework developed by reworking classical anthropological accounts of ritual for contemporary conditions. Drawing most directly on van Gennep's analysis of rites of passage, the method reframes detachment, liminality, and reintegration not as archaic cultural forms, but as structural operations through which orientation can be suspended, recalibrated, and restored under contemporary conditions of saturation. The claim is not that such structures can be straightforwardly re-enacted, nor that contemporary subjects can step outside mediation altogether. Rather, these anthropological patterns are treated as conceptual resources for thinking how instinct—understood as pre-reflective orientation—might be loosened from its algorithmic synchronisation, held in abeyance, and re-formed under conditions that interrupt continuous cueing and predictive saturation. What is at stake is the preservation of originality through the deliberate reintroduction of intervals, thresholds, and transitions through which instinct can again function as orientation rather than as a reflex trained by the stream.

Bibliography

Berardi, F. (2011). *After the future* (G. Genosko & N. Thoburn, Eds). AK Press.

Bergson, H. (1913). *An introduction to metaphysics* (T. E. Hulme, Trans.). Macmillan and Co., Limited. Retrieved from https://ia601508.us.archive.org/12/items/in.ernet.dli.2015.41278/2015.41278.An-Introduction-To-Metaphysics_text.pdf.

Bergson, H. (2001a). The multiplicity OF conscious states the idea of duration. In *Time and free will: An essay on the immediate data of consciousness* (pp. 76–139). Dover Publications.

Bergson, H. (2001b). *Time and free will: An essay on the immediate data of consciousness*. Dover Publications.

Cataldi, S. L. (2008). Affect and sensibility. In R. Diprose & J. Reynolds (Eds.), *Merleau-Ponty: Key concepts* (pp. 163–173). Acumen.

Hume, D. (2003). *A treatise of human nature*. Dover.

Hume, D. (2007). *An enquiry concerning human understanding* (P. J. R. Millican, Ed.). Oxford University Press.

McDowell, J. H. (2003). *Mind and world: With a new introduction* (1. Harvard Univ. Press paperback ed., 8. Print). Harvard Univ. Press.

Polanyi, M. (2009a). Tacit knowing. In *The tacit dimension* (Reproduction en fac-similé) (pp. 1–26). University of Chicago Press.

Polanyi, M. (2009b). *The tacit dimension* (Reproduction en fac-similé). University of Chicago press.

Polanyi, M. (2012). *Personal knowledge* (1st ed.). Taylor and Francis.

Rorty, R. (1979). *Philosophy and the mirror of nature*. Princeton University Press.

Sellars, W. (1997). *Empiricism and the philosophy of mind*. Harvard University Press.

Chapter 5
From Van Gennep to the DIEM Method: A Contemporary Model of Transformation

This present chapter is more speculative in nature than those preceding it. It is less grounded in established traditions and more directly informed by lived experience, fieldwork, and personal reflection drawn from anthropological work.

I do not wish to claim that contemporary societies shall abandon rational infrastructures, nor that alternative forms of orientation can be transplanted wholesale into present conditions. That would be preposterous. Rather, I intend to propose the idea that other ways of organising life—or part of it—and meaning have existed, and still exist, in which explicit, propositional modes of orientations are not treated as sovereign, yet social order, moral intelligibility, and a sense of meaningful life are nevertheless sustained. Anthropological accounts are used here as records of workable forms of life in which orientation proceeds primarily through embodied practice, ritual structure, and shared attunement rather than continuous abstraction and calculation. The task of this chapter is therefore twofold.

First, it aims to demonstrate, through concrete anthropological cases, that embodied and non-propositional modes of orientation—that is, instinctive, pre-reflective forms of knowing and acting that operate beneath and prior to rational abstraction—can function as viable foundations of social life.

Second, it seeks to propose a working approach for loosening overly symbolic and over-rationalised interpretations of experience. What follows is not a universal method or a one-size-fits-all solution, but an approach developed over years of observation, lived engagement, and comparative reflection across different contexts. Drawing selectively on Arnold van Gennep's structure of the rite of passage as a loose analytical blueprint, I use it not as a prescriptive model but as a heuristic device to articulate recurring patterns repeatedly encountered in practice. The aim is not to offer a psychological framework or a therapeutic programme, but to suggest one possible way of easing the compression imposed by excessive symbolic mediation and reopening access to a more immediate, interior orientation. This proposal

L. Loriga, *Instinct, Reason and the Self in the Aftermath of Postmodernity*, SpringerBriefs in Psychology, https://doi.org/10.1007/978-3-032-25339-2_5

should be read as a reflection grounded in lived experience rather than as a formal solution.

5.1 Van Gennep's Tripartite Schema of Embodied Transformation

If we are to reconstruct a practical method for understanding how humans are oriented through non-propositional and embodied forms of knowing, a conceptual blueprint is required—one that does not assume linear progress or purely rational decision-making, but instead attends to moments of disruption, suspension, and reorientation. The examples that follow are deliberately heterogeneous and, at times, intentionally provocative. Their purpose is modest: to show that embodied forms of knowing are neither marginal nor archaic but have repeatedly functioned as stable and meaningful ways of orienting human life. Yet before moving to these examples, the formal structure through which such shifts in orientation occur must be made explicit.

That structure is provided by the work of the French anthropologist Arnold van Gennep.

Writing in the early twentieth century, van Gennep was concerned less with the doctrinal content of religion than with the ritual dynamics by which individuals undergo social and ontological transformation. In *Les Rites de Passage* (1909), he sought to systematise the myriad ceremonies by which people pass from one state of life to another—birth, puberty, marriage, ordination, death—by identifying a formal structure common across cultures and traditions. It is therefore warranted to treat this structure as analytically relevant to the present purpose, insofar as the task is to describe a transition not merely between social roles, but between modes of orientation and forms of knowing, including a shift away from exclusive reliance on explicit rational deliberation toward more embodied and instinctive forms of judgement. Such a structure, consists of three sequential phases and serves as the starting point for the approach proposed here:

> *...a complete scheme of rites of passage theoretically includes preliminal rites (rites of separation), liminal rites (rites of transition), and postliminal rites (rites of incorporation)...* (Van Gennep, 1992, p. 11)

5.1.1 Separation and Liminality as Technologies of Transformation

Separation marks a deliberate rupture from a prior status or mode of being. It is enacted through symbolic detachment: physical removal, bodily alteration, ritual disavowal, or social exclusion. What matters is not the form but the effect—a *disruption* of continuity that breaks the hold of habitual roles, narratives, and expectations. In Hindu society, for example, the Brahman—who van Gennep calls a member of the *twice-born* (Van Gennep, 1992, p. 104)—does not simply inherit priestly status. It must be ritually enacted through a sequence of initiations structured explicitly in tripartite terms:

> *...within the sacred world which the Brahman inhabits from birth there are three compartments: a preliminal one lasting until the upanayana (beginning of a relationship with a teacher), a liminal one (novitiate), and a postliminal one (priesthood).* (Van Gennep, 1992, p. 105)

The preliminal phase involves tonsure, bathing, ritual renaming, and symbolic death: a severing from childhood and from the profane world. Comparable rites of separation recur in Catholic and Orthodox ordination, where the tonsure functions simultaneously as a sign of removal and dedication, and in royal enthronement, where purification, renaming, and withdrawal precede accession to power. In each case, separation is not metaphorical but operative: it destabilises identity by interrupting its continuity.

Yet separation alone does not transform. It opens onto what van Gennep identifies as the most dangerous and generative phase: liminality. The liminal subject exists betwixt and between, no longer what they were, not yet what they will become. Social norms are suspended, identities rendered ambiguous, and ordinary rules temporarily revoked. This phase is structurally unstable and often marked by ordeal, licence, and symbolic death. Among the Subba (Sabians) near Baghdad—van Gennep reports—ecclesiastical advancement requires baptism, seclusion, fasting, ritual death, and resurrection; notably, the investiture of a bishop includes an explicit funeral:

> *On the eighth day a funeral is held for him, since he is considered dead. Afterwards, he is accompanied by four priests to the river, where they administer baptism to him.* (Van Gennep, 1992, p. 107)

The same approach governs shamanic initiation across Siberian and Central Asian traditions. Van Gennep describes a sequence of suffering, possession, withdrawal, visionary training, ritual death, and return, stressing that these elements do not merely symbolise transformation but constitute it:

> *...the shaman dies and his soul departs to the land of the spirits, the gods, or the dead. There he learns its topography and acquires the knowledge necessary to subdue the evil spirits and obtain the assistance of the good ones. The shaman then returns to life, is reborn, and returns home or goes from village to village, and so forth.* (Van Gennep, 1992, p. 108)

Political rites follow the same grammar. In the enthronement of the Dogon hogon, drawing on Augustin-Marie Louis Desplagnes' *Le plateau central nigérien*, van Gennep records that installation entails a ritual social death:

> *...from the time of his entrance in the house of the hogon and his taking possession of the "symbols of union," the servant and high priest of the deity is considered dead to his family.* (Van Gennep, 1992, p. 113)

During liminality, the initiate is structurally anomalous—neither inside nor outside society—and thus exempt from its norms. Among the Vai of Liberia initiates are permitted to steal and pillage during the novitiate (Van Gennep, 1992, p. 138); similar licence characterises Melanesian initiation societies such as the Duk-Duk and Ingiet. This suspension of order is not moral failure but functional necessity: liminality dissolves the taken-for-granted frameworks through which the world is ordinarily apprehended.

Later thinkers clarified further *how* liminality operates at the level of perception and embodiment. Mircea Eliade's analysis of shamanism makes explicit that liminality is a technology of consciousness. The ritualised destruction of the novice's body—being dismembered, boiled, reduced to a skeleton—is not metaphorical but epistemic.

> *Each of these elements in the initiatory story is consistent and has its place in a symbolic or ritual system... they represent a well-organized variant of the universal theme of the death and mystical resurrection of the candidate by means of a descent to the underworld and an ascent to the sky.* (Eliade, 2004, p. 43)

Such a structure recurs everywhere from the Samoyed shamans, whose spirits cut them up and carry their soul to the god Mikkulai, to the Tungus, whose candidates must name the spirits as they enter their body, recounting each spirit's biography and previous incarnations within the tribe. Among the Buryat, the initiate climbs a ritual birch planted in the hearth—an *axis mundi* (Eliade, 2004, p. 239)—while drumming in trance, not to symbolise transcendence but to effect it. In each case, knowledge is not symbolic representation; it is power, presence, and continuity with an invisible order that must be reactivated through ordeal.

5.1.2 Liminality and the Reconfiguration of Perception

This suspension of inherited categories does not merely reorganise social position; it alters perception itself, reshaping how the world is sensed, interpreted, and inhabited. This insight finds a parallel in Christian mystical traditions, where liminality is internalised and rendered solitary rather than communal. Teresa of Ávila's *Interior Castle* describes a progressive stripping away of discursive thought, self-will, and attachment, culminating in a transformation of perception rather than the acquisition of doctrine. She writes:

> *The door of entry to this castle is prayer and reflection. The essential aspect of prayer is attention to God, whether the prayer is vocal or mental.* (St. Teresa of Ávila, 2020, p. 35)

In the Fourth Dwelling Places, she distinguishes between effortful consolation and infused delight, the latter arising without conscious control:

> *This spiritual delight is different from earthly consolations. The delight fills everything, overflowing through all the dwelling places and faculties, until reaching the body... begins in God and ends in ourselves.* (St. Teresa of Ávila, 2020, p. 93)

Here liminality takes the form of sustained unknowing, a suspension of analytic mastery that allows perception itself to be reconfigured. The anonymous author of *The Cloud of Unknowing* articulates this with clarity:

> *He may well be loved, but not thought. By love may he be gotten and holden; but by thought never.* (Anonymous, 1978, p. 39)

Liminality, whether ritual or contemplative, thus entails a deliberate bracketing of inherited categories. It is a descent into uncertainty that functions not as confusion but as reorientation. Teresa gives this logic through the silkworm metaphor, in which transformation is achieved not through refinement but through the deliberate destruction of the former self:

> *Continuing with the silkworm metaphor, Teresa urges the nuns to be quick in weaving their cocoons by getting rid of self-love, self-will, and attachments, and by carrying out the deeds of a good life. Through those things the soul will die to the world and live in God through the prayer of union.* (St. Teresa of Ávila, 2020, p. 127)

Gnostic traditions generalise this logic by extending liminality from a method of transformation to a diagnosis of the world itself. The world is not merely corrupt but fundamentally distorted—a counterfeit reality shaped by ignorance, domination, and illusion. Truth lies not in appearances or institutions but behind them, hidden like a spark in the soul. *Gnosis* is the piercing of that veil—not through explanation or argument, but through a form of recognition that feels less like discovery than remembering.

The Gnostic tradition resisted the institutionalisation of knowledge, offering instead a vision in which the divine is accessed through inward awakening, not ecclesiastical mediation (see, e.g. King, 2003 and also Pagels, 1989). This is not epistemology in the rationalist sense, but a fundamental shift in perception: the soul comes to recognise its estrangement from the world and turns inward, seeking the source of its being beyond the visible order.

5.1.3 Incorporation and the Body as a Site of Knowledge

The final phase of van Gennep's schema is incorporation: the return from liminality into the social world, now transformed. This return does not stabilise transformation at the level of belief alone; it must be sedimented in practice, posture, and comportment—what Marcel Mauss later theorised, in a different context, as *techniques of the body*. Bodily knowledge cannot be grasped abstractly but must be observed in its concrete variations. Bodily knowledge is always enacted through specific practices: how French soldiers dig differently from British ones, how Polynesian swimmers breathe differently from Europeans, how Japanese children learn to squat comfortably for long periods while many Westerners cannot, how infants are taught to sleep across cultures, or how Mediterranean speakers gesture expansively while Northern Europeans keep their hands still.

> *It is essential to move from the concrete to the abstract and not the other way round.* (Mauss, 1973, p. 70)

These bodily capacities feel natural and automatic, yet they are learnt. What appears as spontaneous instinct—how one stands, breathes under stress, or handles a tool—is shaped through years of imitation and practice. This trained responsiveness operates beneath reflective awareness, carrying out countless micro-adjustments without demanding attention. One does not think about how to balance while walking; the body already does it. That prior embodied orientation is what makes deliberate action in the world possible at all. When Marcel Mauss describes French soldiers unable to use British spades because they had learnt to dig differently, or Polynesian swimmers developing breathing techniques unlike Europeans, he shows that even seemingly natural activities are culturally formed. What appears spontaneous is the result of years of training, imitation, and social transmission—what Mauss calls *prestigious imitation* (Mauss, 1973, p. 73) whereby individuals acquire bodily techniques by copying those who carry recognised authority or value. Incorporation is marked by public recognition, regalia, new roles, and renewed obligations. Yet crucially, incorporation does not restore the previous state; it stabilises change. Transformation becomes durable only when it is sedimented in bodily practice: *Techniques* here are '…the ways in which from society to society men know how to use their bodies' (Mauss, 1973, p. 70)—how they walk, rest, carry, swim, endure, suffer, gesture, and regulate effort. These techniques operate below conscious reflection, enabling action without deliberation. They are what allow the initiate to *inhabit* their new status rather than merely understand it. Incorporation, in this sense, is not ideological but somatic: a re-patterning of posture, gesture, perception, and response that renders the transformation liveable.

This somatic re-patterning extends beyond posture and gesture to perception itself—particularly to modes of sensing marginalised by dominant visual and representational epistemologies. Beyond instrumental sound, the voice itself becomes a site of power, particularly in the performance of praise poetry and incantation. Here, meaning arises not from semantic clarity but from the affective and vibrational force of the spoken word. As one healer remarks to Stoller, 'You listen, but you do not hear' (Stoller, 2010, p. 115), signifying that to truly understand, one must attune to the world beyond the analytical level. In this way, language functions not as representation but as action. Incantations, for instance, do not describe power—they enact it. Their force lies in the rhythm, cadence, and breath through which they are delivered, not in referential meaning. Sound, in the Songhay world, is an ontological medium through which the visible and invisible, the social and the spiritual, are fused in dynamic relation. As Stoller notes, '…the eye and its gaze… has had a lockhold on Western thought' (Stoller, 2010, p. 101), whereas among the Songhay, tone, not object, is the medium of knowledge.

Stoller's first-hand ethnography of possession ceremonies hints toward how knowledge in the Songhay context is not transmitted through abstract discourse, but through embodied experience. Instruments such as the *godji* (monochord violin) and *gasi* (gourd drum) are not merely musical tools; they are vehicles for spiritual encounter. The *godji*, with its high-pitched wail often described as a *cry*, evokes the presence of ancestors and stirs both mediums and spirits into action. Its sound is considered sacred—capable of linking present ceremonies to mythic pasts—while the *gasi* produces rhythmic patterns that correspond to the dance movements of mediums and the temperaments of the spirits being invoked.

> *Listen to the godji [violin] and let its cries penetrate you. Then you will know the voice of the spirits, "they would tell me." Feel the sound of the drum and know the power of our past.* (Stoller, 2010, p. 101)

Among Nayaka foragers, approaching a honey tree involves offering, attention, and bodily sensing. Trees are not objects but persons-in-relation. What is known is not universal fact but relational history—how this tree responded last season, to this person, in this weather (Bird-David, 1999; Naveh & Bird-David, 2014). Even among hunters, knowledge develops not through mental modelling but through perceptual reorientation—learning to see as prey sees, to hear as the forest hears. This is not metaphorical, but a disciplined perceptual adjustment. Knowledge here arises from movement, attention, modulation—not from conceptual distance (Kohn, 2013).

A child learning to hunt does not begin with propositions about animal behaviour. They learn by moving through the land with elders, noticing what the elders notice, gradually developing the capacity to read tracks, wind, terrain, and movement as meaningful signs. Knowledge is not stored in the head but enacted through attunement to the world. This logic continues in other domains. Trackers in the Kalahari—a vast semi-arid region spanning Botswana, Namibia, and South Africa—examine prints and infer which animal passed, how long ago, whether injured or fleeing, where it might be found. These are testable inferences—empirical reasoning in the strictest sense—yet conducted without instruments or written records. The tracker's body carries the memory: the capacity to distinguish subtle signs in compressed soil, disturbed grass, or scent. A novice sees marks; an expert sees story. Mushroom foragers seeking matsutake—fungi that cannot be cultivated—do not follow maps or instructions. They read the forest: the undergrowth, light, soil, trees, moisture. Their knowledge is not extractable; it lives in hands, eyes, seasonal rhythms, and communal memory (see, e.g. Tsing et al., 2008; Tsing, 2015). Inuit wayfinding proceeds through bodily engagement with wind, ice, and snow (Aporta, 2009)—reading flex underfoot, noticing snowdrifts shaped by wind, recognising salinity through colour. After years, navigation is no longer cognitive but embodied. When GPS replaces this, something is lost. The device gives answers, but it dissolves attunement. Navigation becomes externalised; the environment no longer teaches. And again, trackers in the Kalahari read soil, grass, and scent not through abstract inference but through embodied attunement (Liebenberg et al., 2021).

In all these cases, incorporation produces not passive conformity but practical agency. The transformed subject returns capable of acting differently, perceiving differently, and resisting forms of orientation that no longer hold.

5.2 The DIEM Method: From Rite of Passage to Contemporary Resistance

Let us now turn to the practical dimension of the argument developed so far. I argued that *separation* functions as rupture, a deliberate break with habitual roles, environments, and orientations. *Liminality* operates as suspension: a descent into unknowing in which inherited assumptions are bracketed and ordinary frames of reference lose their authority. *Incorporation* finally marks return: the stabilisation of change through embodied practice rather than abstract belief. This tripartite structure is not only an anthropological curiosity identified by van Gennep. It is a recurrent grammar of reorientation that appears wherever individuals are compelled—or choose—to reorganise their relation to the world. What varies historically are the modes, conditions, and expressions of transformation, while such underlying tripartite logic reappears. The present conditions are those described in the preceding chapters: symbolic saturation, algorithmic cueing, and the progressive automation of instinct within what I have termed the *Sensorial Nexus*. Orientation is no longer primarily shaped by shared ritual, embodied apprenticeship, or gradual habituation, but by externally mediated systems that pre-arrange salience, relevance, and response at the level of perception itself. The framework proposed here is a practical response to this condition. I therefore propose a method oriented toward introspective transformation rather than collective ritual, not because communal forms have lost their efficacy in principle, but because the task at hand is not external alignment with shared ideologies, norms, or narratives, but the recovery of inner honesty and personal judgement. I call this framework the *DIEM Method.*

The DIEM Method unfolds the tripartite logic of passage into four analytically distinct, yet structurally continuous moments: *Disruptio*, *Introspectio*, *Examen*, and *Manifestatio*. These are not stages to be completed mechanically, nor a universal solution to existential disorientation. They function as an orientation device: a way of loosening inherited symbolic constraints and re-establishing an inner axis of judgement under conditions in which orientation is increasingly outsourced to external systems. The method preserves the first and final movements of van Gennep's schema—rupture and return—largely intact. The emphasis of the DIEM Method lies in its treatment of liminality. What van Gennep describes as a single threshold phase is here analytically unfolded into two distinct moments. *Introspectio* names the sustained exposure to oneself that follows withdrawal: the gradual shedding of social roles, narrative identities, and inherited self-descriptions. *Examen* designates the phase in which this exposed subjectivity is recognised, accepted, and learned—without justification, correction, or idealisation. What follows is not metaphorical description, but a practical articulation of each phase: what it does, how it works, how it is enacted, and how one knows when it has done its work.

5.2.1 *Disruptio: Rupture from the Sensorial Nexus*

Disruptio names the intentional rupture from the structures that quietly organise ordinary life. Under contemporary conditions, those structures are no longer primarily institutional or ideological; they are sensory and algorithmic. Attention, affect, and relevance are continuously shaped by predictive systems that operate prior to reflection. As long as the subject remains embedded within this environment, orientation is already pre-arranged. Disruptio therefore targets exposure rather than interpretation.

Its function is simple: destabilisation, eradication, and collapse. It destabilises habitual orientation, eradicates the scaffolding through which identity and relevance are maintained, and forces the collapse of routines that normally conceal dependency. It deliberately reproduces the condition long recognised in medical anthropology as revelatory: the removal of familiar structures through which reliance, vulnerability, and externally sustained orientation become unmistakably visible. The mechanism of Disruptio is *deprivation*. By suspending habitual roles, inputs, and obligations, it interrupts the feedback loops through which identity and instinct are continuously reinforced. When stimulation is removed, boredom, irritability, anxiety, and disorientation surface. These reactions are not failures; they are diagnostic. They reveal the extent to which orientation has been externally scaffolded. They are withdrawal symptoms.

Disruptio requires concrete, physical withdrawal that violates the assumptions of ordinary life. It is not symbolic distancing, partial reduction, or managed absence, but an enforced severance from the structures that sustain artificial rhythm and relevance.

- Suspend participation in work, productivity, and routine obligations entirely.
- Abandon the habitual environment; leave the city and its infrastructural tempo if at all possible.
- Eliminate all screens, media, news, and digital communication without substitution.
- Reduce social contact to a single emergency channel.
- Strip daily life to its irreducible biological minimum: eating, walking, resting, sleeping.

This withdrawal is deliberately anti-natural in the contemporary sense. It breaks not only habits, but the engineered environments that pass for nature under conditions of permanent connectivity. What remains is not simplicity, but exposure: the subject without scaffolding, rhythm without command, time without instruction.

Disruptio is not successful when distress first appears. Discomfort is expected and diagnostically irrelevant. What matters is the gradual weakening of externally imposed rhythms. In the initial phase, time feels distorted, impulses recur, and the urge to reconnect dominates—much like withdrawal in addiction.

Success begins when those compulsions lose force. External rhythms—notifications, expectations, roles, algorithmic pacing—become perceptible as imposed rather than necessary. They no longer command behaviour with the same urgency. As in detoxification, craving does not vanish abruptly; it thins out. Attention stops snapping back automatically. One can remain without immediately compensating.

Disruptio has done its work when orientation is no longer synchronised to external cueing, when time is no longer structured by demand, and when the performative self—worker, partner, function, mask—ceases to be continuously reactivated. What collapses is not the Self, but the externally intensified dominance of the organised *Me*.

5.2.2 *Introspectio: Suspension of Orientation*

Introspectio names the sustained suspension of orientation that follows rupture. Once external rhythms, cues, and demands have been withdrawn, attention turns inward. This phase is not reflective analysis, but exposure to the subject as it appears when no role, task, or audience is operative. The term subject is used here to designate first-person givenness: what is privately accessible in experience prior to interpretation, justification, or social organisation of conduct.

The function of Introspectio is not self-understanding in the narrative sense, but self-recognition. It reveals who one is when nothing is required, expected, or rewarded. This phase dismantles the illusion that solitude delivers immediacy or authenticity by default. Even in isolation, the subject is not alone. What appears inwardly is a dense assemblage of internalised roles, expectations, and demands. This is not an accidental distortion but the ordinary condition of modern subjectivity.

What presents itself is a layered mask. This mask is not theatrical deception but a practical artefact: a composite structure formed through years of adaptation, obligation, loyalty, ambition, and moral alignment. It is built from social positions and functional identities—worker and provider, caretaker and evaluator, ally and opponent, achiever and moral witness. It is reinforced by repetition and reward rather than truth. Like *papier-mâché*, it is light, composite, and durable, held together by habit rather than coherence. Introspectio confronts the subject with this mask not to denounce it, but to recognise it as a mask. What emerges is not a purified inner voice or authentic essence, but the subject that remains as these layers lose authority: impulses without justification, aversions without excuse, desires without narrative cover. This phase confronts the subject with honesty rather than meaning.

Introspectio is enacted through disciplined mental quieting combined with deliberate, unsparing self-analysis. The aim is not relaxation, insight, or self-care, but the interruption of the internal machinery that continuously narrates, excuses, and manages experience. One begins by refusing to follow the inner voice that explains, plans, moralises, and reassures. This voice is not neutral. It is part of the mask: an organising function shaped by survival, expectation, and social intelligibility.

Once this surface noise weakens, the work becomes confrontational. Introspectio turns into a practice of radical questioning directed against impulses, inherited beliefs, and moral reflexes. Every inclination is treated as suspect. Desires are not expressed but interrogated. Convictions are not affirmed but tested. The subject asks relentlessly: *Why do I want this? Whose recognition does this secure? What fear stabilises this belief? Is this impulse mine, or has it been installed through repetition and reward?* This is not reflective dialogue but dismantling. The task is to strip away assumptions until what remains can no longer justify, explain, or defend itself.

The process is necessarily violent in a conceptual sense. It extirpates social identity by exposing its elements as learned responses rather than expressions of honesty. What is dismantled is not consciousness, but the structure of roles through which the subject has learned to function: the responsible adult, the dependable partner, the competent professional, the morally aligned individual. Each belief is pressed until it either collapses or reveals the interest it protects. Introspectio is therefore not about listening to instinct, but about clearing the ground on which instinct might later speak without contamination.

Introspectio fails when the subject replaces one organising structure with another. Immediate calm, clarity, insight, or self-concept formation indicates substitution rather than exposure. Moral accounting, self-critique, fantasy, and premature reconciliation are signs that the mask has merely been refined, not dismantled.

Success begins when the subject recognises that even in solitude they are accompanied by roles that speak, judge, and demand. The first sign of success is not peace, but discomfort: the recognition that much of what presents itself inwardly is performative. Progress begins when these roles can be named without defence and allowed to fall silent, one by one.

Introspectio has done its work when the mask has been dismantled—when the papier-mâché construction of social identity has been peeled away layer by layer, roles torn off until nothing remains to perform. Functional identities fall away—caretaker, evaluator, achiever, moral actor—and none rushes back to take command. The work is complete when the stripping is finished, when the bleeding has stopped, and what remains can no longer hide behind function or virtue. What remains is the subject encountered without role, without justification, and without protection. This exposure is not gentle. It is unsettling, often unbearable. Introspectio is complete when one finds oneself alone with oneself for the first time—perhaps ever—without the papier-mâché that once stood in its place. From this exposed subject, rather than from the mask, judgement can later be reclaimed.

5.2.3 *Examen: Reclaiming Judgement*

Examen begins only once naked familiarity has been established—once the mask has been recognised, dismantled, and no longer intervenes between the subject and itself. Where *Introspectio* was the work of exposure and subtraction—bringing the mask into view and stripping it away—*Examen* marks the first sustained encounter with what remains once that removal is complete. It is not a continuation of dismantling, but the beginning of examination. The subject now stands alone, not to undo further layers, but to explore the contours, impulses, and dispositions of its own nakedness. *Examen* is the phase in which judgement is recovered through direct confrontation with the instincts, vices, desires, aversions, and capacities that persist once social identity has fallen silent.

The function of *Examen* is not purification, correction, or self-improvement, but unfiltered recognition. Its task is to establish an uncompromised account of who the subject in fact is—how it acts, desires, avoids, and pursues once moral filters and social scripts have been stripped away. Radical honesty here is no longer subtractive but declarative. The subject does not ask who it ought to be, but who it is. Desires are not ranked; impulses are neither justified nor condemned. Vices, compulsions, perversions, fears, resentments, and attractions are acknowledged without sanitisation. Judgement is reclaimed not through moral elevation, but through accuracy. *Examen* requires confrontation without mediation:

- Suspension of performative orientation, allowing inclinations, reactions, and behavioural tendencies to appear without being shaped by anticipation of response, approval, or consequence. The aim is not behavioural change, but exposure of preference.
- Refusal of self-explanation, not because motives are unknowable, but because explanation domesticates exposure. No reasons are supplied for desire or avoidance; no contextual accounts are invoked to soften what appears. What arises is allowed to stand as fact.

The task of *Examen* is not restraint, discipline, or reform, but honesty.

Examen fails when the subject retreats into moral accounting, psychological explanation, or aesthetic self-description. Any attempt to redeem, excuse, normalise, or intellectualise desire signals avoidance. Shame-driven suppression and pride-driven idealisation are equally disqualifying. If impulses are filtered to preserve dignity, *Examen* has been abandoned.

Success begins when the subject can state its inclinations—however unflattering, excessive, or disturbing—without defence, apology, or recoil; when desire can be named without justification, and aversion without moralisation; when the subject ceases to flinch at its own inventory.

Examen has done its work when the subject can finally remain alone with itself, without mask, without narrative shelter, and without the need to correct what is found. When it knows, without mitigation or illusion, what it is capable of being and desiring. This is brutal honesty at its highest resolution—not acceptance in the therapeutic sense, but recognition without refusal. Judgement no longer feels borrowed from norms, ideals, or external authorities, because it arises from direct contact with fact.

5.2.4 *Manifestatio: Return Without Automation*

Manifestatio names the return to the social world without reintegration into its dominant orienting structures. The subject re-enters a world still governed by the *Sensorial Nexus*—algorithmic cueing, symbolic saturation, predictive salience—without surrendering orientation to it. This is not withdrawal, refusal, or opposition, but a changed mode of participation. The subject is present in the system without being absorbed by it.

This return does not restore the pre-existing subject. It marks the emergence of a subject capable of acting from within the world without being organised by it. The flow of influence reverses: where orientation was once absorbed passively from external cues, it is now generated internally and projected outward through action.

The function of *Manifestatio* is the stabilisation of truth in action. What was uncovered through rupture (*Disruptio*), stripped bare through suspension (*Introspectio*), and named without illusion (*Examen*) must now be made operative. Without this return, honesty remains private and sterile.

Manifestatio converts naked recognition into responsibility. It is not autonomy in the political or metaphysical sense, but authorship in the strictest sense: the assumption of full responsibility for one's own life and for every action taken within it, without appeal to systems, scripts, roles, or excuses. Instinct—previously automated by the Sensorial Nexus—is restored as embodied orientation rather than reflex. One no longer responds to everything. Indifference becomes possible. What remains is necessity. When something matters, it matters without calculation, without optimisation, and without alternatives. Action ceases to be speculative. It becomes a manifestation of reality, not a preference among options.

Manifestatio requires concrete, irreversible commitments that anchor orientation in the world:

- Re-entry into social systems without submission to them. The subject resumes participation in work, relationships, and institutions, but no longer from passivity or identification. Externally, behaviour may appear unchanged; internally, orientation is reversed. The subject plays the system knowingly instead of being shaped, paced, or governed by it.
- Re-encountering the world without inherited scripts, approaching situations without optimisation or anticipatory conformity. Attraction and aversion are registered directly, not filtered through expectation, status, or reward.
- Withdrawal from acting on behalf of others' expectations. Roles, obligations, and trajectories that exist primarily to secure recognition, approval, or reassurance are relinquished—not as rebellion, but as refusal to continue living through borrowed motives.
- Deliberate reduction of exposure and responsiveness. Participation is narrowed rather than optimised. Availability is limited. Pace is reclaimed. What was uncovered during Introspectio and Examen is actively protected through selective engagement and continual reassessment of what genuinely warrants attention and effort.

These actions are not symbolic gestures. They are cuts that alter the conditions under which future choices will be made.

Manifestatio fails when the subject re-enters the world only to reconstruct the mask—reapplying its layers under the pressure of algorithmic governance and social expectation. Failure sets in the moment the subject begins to re-internalise the generalised social gaze, reinstating the panopticon of self-discipline through the imagined eyes of others. Relapse occurs when one bends again to external will or begins to narrate the world through a newly refined mask. Insight without consequence, clarity without cost, and critique without commitment are all signs of failure. If participation remains governed by visibility, validation, or strategic positioning, the Sensorial Nexus has regained control.

Success begins when action is no longer reactive. When the subject no longer sticks to the world like adhesive—absorbing signals, moods, urgencies—but moves through it without residue. The surfaces of the Sensorial Nexus lose their grip. Notifications, trends, metrics, and ambient demands no longer attach themselves to the subject's interior. Orientation becomes self-sustaining. At this point, intention awakens. Not as ambition, but as necessity. The subject no longer drifts within symbolic currents; it begins to exert directional force. Where once it absorbed meaning, it now transmits.

Manifestatio has done its work when the subject can act from itself without needing confirmation, explanation, or narrative cover. When participation no longer compromises honesty. When instinct—tested, refined, and stripped of illusion—guides action with precision. The spectacle continues. Systems persist. The Sensorial Nexus remains operational. But the subject is no longer inside it. It is no longer played by the game, but plays it knowingly, actively, and at a distance. One participates without surrender, acts without illusion, and remains fully responsible for every choice made.

5.3 Conclusion: DIEM as Resistance

This chapter began with a deliberately modest claim: that rational sovereignty is not the only workable basis for orientation, moral intelligibility, or a meaningful life. Human beings have long relied on embodied practice, apprenticeship, ritual structure, and shared attunement to orient themselves in the world, often beneath propositional modes of orientation and sometimes in direct suspension of it. Van Gennep's tripartite schema clarifies the underlying grammar of shifts in orientation: separation as rupture, liminality as suspension, and incorporation as return, where change becomes durable only when sedimented in embodied practice rather than abstract belief.

What has shifted under contemporary conditions is not this grammar of transformation, but the environment in which orientation is now formed. The Sensorial Nexus does not merely surround the subject with symbols or information; it organises perception itself. Through algorithmic cueing, predictive feeds, and continuous micro-prompts, it pre-arranges salience—what appears urgent, what feels relevant, what is rewarded with attention, and what quietly disappears. Over time, this does not simply distract. It externalises judgement, trains reflex, and automates instinct. Orientation is no longer refined through lived contact with reality; it is progressively outsourced to engineered stimulus–response loops.

The DIEM Method—Disruptio, Introspectio, Examen, Manifestatio—is proposed as a practical counter-form to this condition. It is not a therapeutic programme, a spiritual technique, or a project of self-optimisation. It is a discipline of resistance. More precisely, it is an objection to being governed at the level of perception, affect, and relevance. DIEM does not reject technology as such; it refuses the quiet conversion of the subject into a responsive node whose instincts are trained by algorithmic reinforcement rather than consequence.

DIEM adapts van Gennep's structure into a solitary model suited to the present problem: not external alignment with collective ideology, but the recovery of inner honesty and personal judgement in a world that increasingly dissolves both. Disruptio targets exposure. It breaks the engineered rhythms that organise everyday life and reveals dependency by removing the scaffolding. Introspectio extends liminality into sustained suspension, refusing replacement frameworks so that borrowed orientation is not simply swapped for a new script. Examen reclaims judgement through confrontation: instincts, vices, desires, and aversions are accepted without excuse, performance, or moral varnish, until responsibility becomes factual rather than theatrical. Manifestatio completes the return—not as reintegration into the Sensorial Nexus, but as re-entry without surrender.

At its core, the DIEM Method is a means of re-finding instinct as a lived orientation rather than a reflex trained by systems. This cannot be achieved through refinement, moderation, or propositional correction. It requires purging: the systematic removal of borrowed narratives, moral filters, and algorithmically cued relevance through absolute and brutal self-honesty. Only by suspending propositional modes of orientation—explanation, justification, optimisation—can instinct re-emerge as a reliable signal rather than a conditioned response. The Sensorial Nexus does not eliminate instinct; it replaces it with refined algorithmic cueing that mimics intuition while hollowing it out. DIEM aims to break that substitution by clearing the ground entirely, forcing orientation to arise from direct contact with oneself and the world, rather than from predictive systems designed to bypass judgement altogether.

The point is not escape, purity, or nostalgia for premodern forms of living. It is to recover an inner axis under conditions that systematically dissolve it. Where the Sensorial Nexus trains reflex, DIEM cultivates instinct. Where contemporary governance stabilises drift through continuous cueing, DIEM restores orientation through rupture, suspension, confrontation, and return. And where modern life increasingly treats the subject as something to be managed through prompts, metrics, and optimisation, DIEM insists on an older and more demanding requirement: to become the author of one's own actions and fully responsible for the life one is, in fact, living.

DIEM is therefore not a method of withdrawal, but a method of non-compliance from within. However abstract its present formulation may appear, it offers a way to participate without surrender, to act without illusion, and to resist automation at the only level where it is now decisive: the formation of instinct itself.

Bibliography

Anonymous. (1978). *The cloud of unknowing and other works* (C. Wolters, Ed.). Penguin Books.

Aporta, C. (2009). The trail as home: Inuit and their pan-arctic network of routes. *Human Ecology, 37*(2), 131–146. https://doi.org/10.1007/s10745-009-9213-x

Bird-David, N. (1999). "Animism" revisited: Personhood, environment, and relational epistemology. *Current Anthropology, 40*(S1), S67–S91. https://doi.org/10.1086/200061

Eliade, M. (2004). *Shamanism: Archaic techniques of ecstasy*. Princeton University Press.

King, K. L. (2003). *What is gnosticism?* Harvard University Press.

Kohn, E. (2013). *How forests think: Toward an anthropology beyond the human*. University of California Press.

Liebenberg, L., //Ao, A. M., Lombard, M., Shermer, M., Xhukwe, U., Biesele, M., //Xao, D., Carruthers, P., Kxao, O., Hansson, S. O., Langwane, H. (Karoha), Elbroch, L. M., Ui, N., Keeping, D., Humphrey, G., Newman, G., G/aq'o, U., Steventon, J., Kashe, N., et al. (2021). Tracking science: An alternative for those excluded by citizen science. *Citizen Science: Theory and Practice, 6*(1), 6. https://doi.org/10.5334/cstp.284

Mauss, M. (1973). Techniques of the body. *Economy and Society, 2*(1), 70–88. https://doi.org/10.1080/03085147300000003

Naveh, D., & Bird-David, N. (2014). How persons become things: Economic and epistemological changes among Nayaka hunter-gatherers. *Journal of the Royal Anthropological Institute, 20*(1), 74–92. https://doi.org/10.1111/1467-9655.12080

Pagels, E. H. (1989). *The gnostic gospels*. Vintage Books.

St. Teresa of Ávila. (2020). *The interior castle* (K. Kavanaugh & O. Rodríguez, Trans.; Study edition. 2nd ed.). ICS Publications.

Stoller, P. (2010). *The taste of ethnographic things: The senses in anthropology*. University of Pennsylvania Press.

Tsing, A. L. (2015). *The mushroom at the end of the world: On the possibility of life in capitalist ruins*. Princeton University Press.

Tsing, A. L., Satsuka, S., & for the Matsutake Worlds Research Group. (2008). Diverging understandings of forest management in matsutake science. *Economic Botany, 62*(3), 244–253. https://doi.org/10.1007/s12231-008-9035-6

Van Gennep, A. (1992). *The rites of passage* (M. B. Vizedom & G. L. Caffee, Trans.; 12. print). Univ. of Chicago Press.

Chapter 6
The Future After Collapse

It is now time to draw the conclusions of what has been argued so far. This chapter ends the book and is divided into three sections. In the first, I summarise the points developed in the preceding sections in order to render the central claim fully explicit in its structure and implications. In the second, I outline possible objections to my line of reasoning, acknowledging that the argument advanced here is by no means beyond challenge. Finally, I offer some concluding reflections that follow from the position defended throughout this work.

6.1 The Central Claim

This book began with a simple concern: the erosion of mentorship in a world that no longer felt coherent. That concern, pursued through historical and philosophical analysis, gradually unfolded into a wider diagnosis of our contemporary condition.

I began by arguing that mentorship—the capacity to recognise the nuances of a pupil and cultivate them so that they might unfold and mature organically—presupposes a stable orientation. Such orientation historically relied on shared narratives and, in the Western world, on reason as a navigational tool operating within those narratives. Tradition functioned as a living, embodied framework anchoring identity, meaning, and judgement. The crisis of this orientation was brought into explicit focus by postmodern critique, which articulated a double movement already underway: the historical erosion of tradition and the cognitive expansion of reflective, symbol-mediated reason. Through early modern philosophy, the Enlightenment project of autonomous reason, subsequent positivist rationality, technological mediation, and the rise of capitalist and bureaucratic systems, inherited frameworks were progressively displaced. Authority shifted from tradition to self-grounding reason; what had once been received became something to justify, reconstruct, or discard.

L. Loriga, *Instinct, Reason and the Self in the Aftermath of Postmodernity*, SpringerBriefs in Psychology, https://doi.org/10.1007/978-3-032-25339-2_6

At the same time, cognition increasingly started operating through abstraction and symbolic mediation. Instinct and reason—understood here broadly as non-propositional and propositional modes of orientation—once functioned as complementary dimensions of human knowing. Instinct names those forms of sensing, responding, and finding one's bearings that precede abstraction; reason refers to the capacity to relate to the world through articulated claims and justifications. Over time, however, the balance shifted decisively in favour of reason. As reflective and symbolic capacities intensified, doubt became structural. The widening gap between impulse and interpretation enabled critical distance and reflective self-awareness, but it also introduced hesitation, fragmentation, and interpretive instability. Such reflexivity and fragmentation gradually collapsed into a single temporal condition in which consciousness lags behind the speed of stimulus. Under conditions of acceleration—namely, the increasing velocity and density of signals within digitally mediated environments, where cyberspace, the boundless expansion of digital circulation, collides with cybertime, the finite, embodied capacity of attention to process experience—reflective judgement increasingly arrives too late. The speed of signals outpaces the duration required for integration. Deliberation becomes retrospective commentary on impulses already triggered within compressed cycles of stimulation and response. When reflective integration can no longer keep pace with the velocity of signals, representation begins to detach from lived reference. What circulates is no longer anchored in experience but in repetition and amplification.

Drawing on Baudrillard, I argued that this detachment culminates in hyperreality: signs no longer point to an underlying reality but generate self-contained systems of circulation. The distinction between the real and its representation collapses. This dynamic extends beyond media into everyday life. Identity shifts from inheritance to lifestyle; embodiment becomes curated and metricised; subjectivity becomes performative. Individuals no longer inhabit roles but enact them under constant visibility and evaluation. In this environment of continuous exposure and performance, the classical panoptic model of surveillance mutates into a diffuse and internalised form. Control no longer depends primarily on prohibition or external discipline, but on voluntary exposure, self-optimisation, and continuous visibility. The subject internalises evaluation not as repression but as opportunity—a form of Promethean freedom that promises limitless self-construction while quietly intensifying self-monitoring; *the subject burning itself as fuel for its own projects,* as phrased previously. This marked an epistemic shift in how reality is encountered and processed. Under technological and computational imperatives, language increasingly served performativity rather than truth. Knowledge is valued for optimisation and operational output rather than grounding or meaning. Grand narratives lost authority; justification gave way to execution; deliberation was displaced by metrics. The cultural shift is therefore not from freedom to constraint, but from prohibition to positivity. Power no longer says *you must not*; it says *you can*—and in doing so generates compulsive productivity, perpetual responsiveness, and the exhaustion of interior space.

Within this destabilised landscape, Artificial Intelligence (AI) marked a qualitative intensification. AI did not initiate the collapse of reference; it operationalised it and added momentum to it. Meaning became statistical approximation rather than lived participation. Judgement, already weakened philosophically, is now increasingly deferred to technical systems. Reflection risks displacement by automated suggestion. From this consideration I proposed a further claim: we are no longer simply within postmodernity but in its aftermath. Postmodernity completed its task of dismantling foundations—truth, narrative coherence, stable identity. What followed is not liberation but drift, increasingly stabilised and managed by technical systems. Critique gave way to procedure. Meaning is no longer contested; it is operationally organised. Postmodernity therefore has exhausted itself; its incredulity toward metanarratives has become background common sense. The vacuum it produced has been filled by digital infrastructures organising relevance and response in advance, so that salience itself becomes engineered rather than discovered.

Two further points followed. The first is that saturation—of information, stimuli, and symbolic demands under conditions of digital acceleration—has produced dependency. Under acceleration and cognitive overload, technological integration has ceased to be optional. Human agency increasingly functions within tightly coupled biological–technical systems. Second, these developments converge in what I have termed the *Sensorial Nexus*: a condition in which symbolic mediation, algorithmic governance, and infrastructural anticipation operate at the level of perception itself. The issue is no longer only what we think, but what appears salient before we think. The Sensorial Nexus therefore operates pre-reflectively: it shapes not only judgement but the field within which judgement becomes possible at all.

Drawing on Mead's distinction between the *I* and the Me—the spontaneous, initiating dimension of the self (the I) and the internalised social perspective that organises conduct (the Me)—I then argued that the generalised other, once formed through stable social interaction, within the Sensorial Nexus is now algorithmically curated. The *Me* becomes shaped by continuously updated streams of engineered social attitudes. More provocatively, this shaping extends into pre-reflective orientation itself, influencing what becomes perceptually available and affectively charged. Subjectivity remains privately accessible yet increasingly formed by external systems. Freedom does not disappear, but the interval in which novelty and refusal can arise narrows. Agency becomes attenuated. What is compressed is not metaphysical freedom, but the interval between stimulus and endorsement—the narrow space within which hesitation, refusal, and originality once emerged.

Against this, I defended the philosophical legitimacy of instinct. The appeal to non-propositional modes of orientation is neither nostalgic nor anti-rational. Drawing on Bergson, Hume, and Polanyi, I proposed that analytic reason spatialises and symbolises becoming, grasping lived duration only retrospectively. Intuition, understood as disciplined coincidence with inner movement, complements conceptual reconstruction. I further suggested that reason cannot generate action, moral salience, or belief without prior habit and sentiment. Finally, I extended this proposal into epistemology: explicit knowledge depends upon tacit, embodied integration. Attempts to render all-knowing fully explicit result in destructive analysis, dissolving the integrations that make judgement possible.

The point of this excursus was to drive toward a single conclusion: instinct—understood as intuition, habit, tacit knowing, embodied responsiveness—is the enabling ground of orientation. Postmodernity destabilised the authority of reason; the *Sensorial Nexus* does not restore that loss but intensifies it by pre-structuring perception itself. Under these conditions, instinct is not eliminated but overwritten. It is compressed into reflex and synchronised with external cues. What appears as intuition risks becoming conditioned responsiveness: a form of automated attunement trained by predictive systems rather than by lived consequence. The danger is not irrationality but anthropological distortion: the displacement of situated judgement by pre-structured responsiveness.

As my own contribution—and as a form of resistance to the algorithmic pre-structuring of the *Sensorial Nexus*, that is, perception, and thereby of instinct itself—I proposed a speculative yet practical framework. Through anthropological cases, I meant to show that embodied and non-propositional forms of orientation have long sustained meaningful social life. Drawing on van Gennep's tripartite schema—separation, liminality, incorporation—I reformulated a recurring grammar of transformation: rupture from prior orientation, suspension of inherited frameworks, and return through embodied re-patterning. This structure was adapted into a contemporary model suited to the *Sensorial Nexus*: *the DIEM Method—Disruptio, Introspectio, Examen, Manifestatio*. Disruptio interrupts engineered rhythms and exposes dependency. Introspectio suspends inherited roles and dismantles the performative mask. Examen confronts desire and disposition without justification, reclaiming judgement through radical honesty. Manifestatio stabilises this orientation through action and responsibility without surrender to external cueing, by deliberately reintroducing rupture, suspension, and embodied re-patterning into a world otherwise governed by continuous cueing and temporal compression.

My overall intention should by now be clear. The crisis of mentorship, from which the idea of this book is born, reveals a deeper crisis of orientation. That crisis arises from the erosion of tradition, the overextension of reason, and the algorithmic reorganisation of perception. Reason alone cannot restore direction because it presupposes a pre-reflective ground it cannot generate. Moreover, it is historically weakened by the subtraction of the very faculty from which it emerges and upon which it depends: instinct. Instinct, properly understood, is that ground. Reason and instinct were never enemies but complementary modes of orientation. The elevation of reason at the expense of instinct destabilised reason itself once its inherited ground in tradition was removed. What was long dismissed as animal, pre-rational, or inferior now appears as the enabling condition of judgement. Yet instinct today is not simply neglected; it is being reshaped and synchronised through algorithmic cueing within the Sensorial Nexus.

The task I have sought to propose in this work is therefore not the abandonment of rational life, nor a nostalgic return to premodern forms, but the recovery of instinct as the embodied condition that allows reason, judgement, and responsibility to operate in time. The DIEM Method is my own contribution to this task: modest, provisional, and inevitably incomplete, yet nonetheless a disciplined attempt to enact that recovery under contemporary conditions—before orientation is fully synchronised with the machinery of the Sensorial Nexus and the interval for refusal is reduced beyond recognition.

6.2 Addressing Objections

It is now appropriate to address a number of potential objections that might be reasonably raised against this work. The concerns examined in this section do not exhaust all the weaknesses or tensions in the book. Rather, they represent an attempt to anticipate the most significant ones and to clarify points that may have remained insufficiently explicit in the preceding chapters. I tackle five criticisms and offer explanations accordingly. I will address respectively the alleged romanticisation of tradition; the coherence and explanatory scope of postmodernity and the role attributed to Artificial Intelligence; the novelty and depth of the *Sensorial Nexus* thesis; the reliability of instinct; and the practical viability and ethical defensibility of the *DIEM Method*. Let us now proceed in order.

6.2.1 The Romanticisation of Tradition

The first potential critique concerns the possible accusation that the argument presented here exaggerates the stabilising function of tradition—presenting it as a form of social glue that ensured coherence and intelligibility. A critic might object that so-called premodern societies were not harmonious worlds of shared meaning, but environments structured by violence, exclusion, theological dogma, and rigid hierarchy. Tradition did not merely anchor life; it constrained mobility, suppressed dissent, and naturalised inequality. It may further be argued that doubt and symbolic mediation are not uniquely modern phenomena. The erosion in question is therefore not a simple loss of stability, but a transformation in how meaning is organised. What is at stake is not the disappearance of belief, but the displacement of overarching cosmological frameworks—religious, metaphysical, and communal—by industrial, bureaucratic, and later technocratic structures that reorganise life around production, efficiency, and optimisation rather than shared metaphysical narratives. Under this reading, the argument risks being interpreted as framing modernity as degeneration rather than structural reconfiguration.

My rebuttal here is that the argument I meant to develop is neither nostalgic nor revivalist; it does not advocate a return to traditional forms of life. I do not wish to claim that tradition was, or is, morally superior, socially just, or epistemically infallible. My claim is structural rather than normative. Tradition functioned as an orienting framework: it provided stable symbolic coordinates through which meaning, authority, and expectation were distributed. Stability of orientation does not entail moral goodness. Acknowledging oppression within traditional structures does not negate their orienting function. One may criticise their content while recognising their cognitive and cultural role in stabilising interpretation and action. Doubt is not new. What distinguishes late modernity is not the emergence of reflection, but its saturation and detachment from shared symbolic anchors. The thesis is therefore not that reflection began in modernity, but that it expanded beyond stabilising frameworks. My argument concerned structural change: when inherited frameworks weaken while reflective-symbolic mediation proliferates, instability increases. Recognising the structural function tradition once performed allows its erosion to be analysed conceptually, rather than interpreted nostalgically or romanticised retrospectively.

6.2.2 On Postmodernity and Artificial Intelligence

A further criticism concerns my interpretation of postmodernity and Artificial Intelligence. The objection has three dimensions: the risk of oversimplification, the methodological danger of totalisation, and the question of human agency.

First, the analysis may be read as overstating the coherence and totality of postmodernity, as though consumer culture, simulation, self-tracking, algorithmic mediation, and large language models formed a single, unified trajectory of decline. To gather these heterogeneous and historically uneven phenomena under one interpretive frame risks collapsing complexity into a grand explanatory narrative. The accusation would thus go that my argument constructs an overarching schema out of developments that are fragmented, contradictory, and context-dependent. Second, there is a methodological concern. Postmodern thought itself is critical of totalising explanations—of single frameworks that claim to subsume complex social and epistemic realities under one organising logic. If the present account were to portray postmodernity as a monolithic condition determining subjectivity wholesale, it would reproduce precisely the kind of explanatory gesture that postmodernism sought to dismantle. Third, the objection concerns also agency. Individuals are not merely passive recipients of algorithmic systems. They resist, reinterpret, subvert, and strategically employ digital infrastructures. Artificial Intelligence, in many contexts, augments deliberation, expands access to information, and assists judgement. To describe it primarily as destabilising risks underestimating human reflexivity and overestimating technological determination.

My reply to such line of reasoning is that I use the term postmodernity here diagnostically. It names a dominant configuration in the organisation of meaning, not a uniform or universally determining condition. My analysis concerns structural tendencies and prevailing logic, not total determinations of experience. Where I suggest that we are now *beyond* postmodernity, this should not be read as a dramatic historical rupture or a catastrophic claim that nothing remains to be dismantled. Rather, it marks an intensification and operationalisation of postmodern fragmentation within technological infrastructures. The argument is not apocalyptic. Agency, reflexivity, and resistance remain possible—indeed, this entire project presupposes their continued viability. The claim is more limited: the conditions under which orientation stabilises have become increasingly fragile. Fragmentation, acceleration, and saturation do not eliminate judgement; they complicate its consolidation and endurance. Artificial Intelligence is not described as inherently corrupting. Nor is epistemic instability treated as a purely postmodern invention. Elements of fragmentation, performativity, and procedural validation have long accompanied human symbolic life. What AI does is formalise, scale, and accelerate these tendencies within systems designed for optimisation and prediction. It does not create instability *ex nihilo*; it operationalises and intensifies structural dynamics already present. The thesis is therefore not that truth disappears. It is that criteria of validation increasingly shift from metaphysical grounding to performance, optimisation, and systemic coherence. This transformation has structural consequences and may carry metaphysical implications insofar as it reshapes how reality is authorised and experienced. However, it does not deny the existence of reality itself. Questions concerning the ontological status of the real were deliberately left unaddressed, as a full treatment would have diverted the scope of this book elsewhere. The concern here is not with what reality is in metaphysical terms, but with the conditions under which claims about reality are authorised, stabilised, and rendered legitimate within contemporary systems. Finally, the emphasis on vulnerability is methodological rather than deterministic. Diagnosis precedes reorientation. To identify imbalance is not to endorse technological fatalism, nor to deny human agency. It is to clarify the altered conditions within which judgement, responsibility, and orientation must now operate.

6.2.3 On the Sensorial Nexus

The novel concept of the Sensorial Nexus is perhaps the most exposed to criticism, not only because it is presented for the very first time in this work, but because it may be seen as overstating algorithmic penetration while underestimating human plasticity. Mediation has always shaped subject formation. Theories of extended cognition suggest that reliance on external scaffolds is constitutive of human cognition rather than evidence of its erosion. What is described here as attenuation of subjectivity might therefore be interpreted instead as reconfiguration or even enhancement of it. The claim that algorithmic systems pattern pre-reflective readiness may appear speculative or overly deterministic.

My reply to such criticism is that the argument presented in this work does not claim that mediation is new. Human cognition has always been scaffolded by tools, symbols, institutions, and technologies. The thesis concerns not the existence of mediation, but the unprecedented temporal density, anticipatory structure, and optimisation logic of contemporary systems. The claim is not one of total colonisation, but of compression. The interval within which deviation—what Mead termed the I—can stabilise itself is narrowed under conditions of continuous cueing and predictive modulation. The issue is not that reflection becomes impossible, but that its temporal margin is reduced. The concern therefore is not tool use as such, nor the externalisation of cognition per se. Extended cognition is not denied. Rather, the question is one of asymmetry. Contemporary scaffolds are designed, optimised, and owned within concentrated technological architectures whose primary aims are not epistemic neutrality or shared deliberation, but engagement, retention, and behavioural prediction. The scaffolding is no longer passive support; it is anticipatory and strategically engineered. The Sensorial Nexus therefore names a shift from episodic mediation to ambient, continuous, and anticipatory modulation. It describes a structural reorganisation of attentional environments. This is not a claim of technological determinism, although it approaches that threshold. I do not advance it to that extent, for if agency were wholly determined by technological architectures, then any appeal to resistance—including the proposal of the DIEM Method—would indeed be futile and reduced to a merely rhetorical gesture. The argument instead concerns altered conditions of salience within which agency now operates. It maintains that orientation is increasingly shaped in advance of reflection, but not that it is thereby rendered impossible.

6.2.4 On Instinct

The proposal of instinct as an umbrella term for embodied and non-propositional modes of orientation may appear vulnerable to a further criticism. It risks romanticising instinct and underestimating the dangers inherent in non-reflective orientation. Pre-reflective knowing—habit, intuition, tacit integration—is not only the enabling ground of judgement; it is also a well-documented source of bias, prejudice, tribalism, and error. The limitation of reason does not in itself justify elevating instinct as corrective. Moreover, it may be argued that algorithmic systems, precisely because they are less affectively entangled, can in certain contexts outperform human intuition. The danger, then, is that the argument merely replaces one fragile faculty with another.

It is necessary to restate my premises with precision. Instinct is not opposed to reason. This point has been made repeatedly and bears repetition. The argument does not displace reason in favour of instinct; it restores their structural relation. Pre-reflective orientation is temporally prior and functionally necessary for judgement, but it is not epistemically sovereign. Reason remains indispensable for articulation, correction, and critique. Instinct is historically formed, socially shaped, and technologically modifiable. It is trainable and distortable. It can be cultivated or corrupted. For that reason, it cannot be trusted blindly. The proposal is not a call to spontaneity or impulsiveness, but to disciplined recalibration. The critique advanced in this work does not target algorithmic systems as such. Nor does it deny that they may outperform unaided intuition in particular tasks. The issue is not computational efficiency. It is agency. The concern arises where salience is pre-shaped unilaterally by opaque systems whose operations are not reciprocally contestable. The question, therefore, is whether tacit orientation remains corrigible through embodied encounter, lived consequence, and reflective integration or whether it becomes progressively optimised within architectures that anticipate response in advance of deliberation. Instinct, as employed here, names the pre-reflective ground upon which reason operates. Its rehabilitation is not a rejection of rationality, but a condition for its meaningful exercise.

6.2.5 On the DIEM Method

The DIEM Method is the final and perhaps most provocative proposal advanced in this work, alongside the concept of the Sensorial Nexus. A possible objection is that it may appear elitist, impractical, or psychologically hazardous. It may be described as elitist insofar as extended withdrawal, interruption of work, and radical self-exposure seem feasible only for those with economic security, temporal flexibility, or relative social insulation. It may appear impractical because modern life is structured around professional, familial, and institutional obligations that cannot simply be suspended at will. It may be judged psychologically hazardous because deliberate dismantling of identity, prolonged solitude, and uncompromising confrontation with oneself may destabilise rather than clarify. Traditional rites of passage were socially scaffolded, communally recognised, and normatively contained. DIEM, by contrast, is solitary and self-administered and may therefore risk alienation, detachment, or self-absorption disguised as authenticity.

The DIEM Method is presented consistently as a method, but one operating at a structural rather than procedural level. It is not a practical handbook prescribing uniform behavioural steps. It articulates an underlying grammar of transformation. Its claim to universality does not concern specific techniques, but the tripartite logic identified by van Gennep and repeatedly observed across cultures: interruption, suspension, and reintegration. If genuine transformation occurs, some form of rupture, liminality, and return must take place. That grammar may be regarded as universal in structure, though not in form. The method does not prescribe one fixed implementation. Its concrete enactment may vary according to context, resources, and psychological capacity. The outer form is adaptable; the structural logic remains constant. DIEM therefore operates at a high level of abstraction while allowing its practical expression to differ across circumstances. Furthermore, the proposal is not speculative invention detached from lived reality. It emerges from anthropological participation, observation, and reflective engagement with concrete practices of transformation encountered in fieldwork and lived contexts. It is distilled from experience rather than imposed upon it. Disruption may be calibrated in duration and intensity. What matters is not extremity, but sufficient structural discontinuity to interrupt automated orientation. The underlying theme remains transformation through interruption, suspension, and return. It is equally necessary to respond to the accusations of elitism and impracticality in direct terms. The DIEM Method does not presuppose privilege; it presupposes priority. Every life is structured by commitments, obligations, and constraints. The decisive question is not whether interruption is possible in absolute terms, but whether it is considered important enough to be made possible in relative terms. If reorientation is not undertaken, it is because other pursuits—security, recognition, productivity, stability—are judged more urgent. That judgement may be reasonable; but it is a judgement nonetheless. Interruption does not require theatrical abandonment of one's life. It requires that space be created where orientation can be confronted. Whether that space is minimal or extended depends on circumstance. The grammar remains constant; the scale varies. To describe the method as elitist is to assume that transformation is a luxury rather than a decision about what matters most. As for psychological hazard, DIEM is not psychotherapy, nor a medical intervention. It does not treat pathology and should not be confused with clinical practice. It is a call to radical honesty. Such honesty may unsettle, but discomfort is not pathology. The method offers no promise of comfort or ease. It proposes responsibility. Whether one chooses to undertake it is, ultimately, a matter of priority.

6.3 Final Remarks

I wish to conclude this work with a personal observation. We live through our bodies and experience the world through our bodies. They are our primary means of perception, even if one were to entertain speculation about transcendental elements interwoven with them. We are bodies in space and time, and as such everything around us actively conditions the modalities through which we perceive the world, through which we feel things as urgent, threatening, intimate, forgettable, or otherwise significant. Precisely because we are embodied in a shared environment—leaving aside, for the moment, the metaphysical question of what shared reality ultimately entails—these conditioning structures are not purely private. They operate across bodies. We are all part of a distributed cognitive architecture, one that patterns perceptual and affective response, if we let them. Such structured perceptual environments can produce statistically significant synchronisation in brain activity across individuals, suggesting that with sufficient formal control, one is able of '...turning them [multiple brain regions] on and off at the same time across all viewers may provide neuroscientific evidence for his notoriously famous ability to master and manipulate viewers' minds' (Hasson et al., 2008, p. 16). This synchronisation is not uniformly present across all forms of perceptual input but varies depending on compositional features. A tightly structured sequence of events can evoke shared cortical responses across nearly half of the neocortex, while an unstructured, continuous segment of real-life input provokes far less intersubject correlation (ISC), namely, '...an emerging metric in cognitive neuroscience, reflects the similarity of neural responses among multiple individuals engaged in the same task' (Liu et al., 2025, p. 1)—and engages only low-level sensory areas. What this implies is that sequencing, framing, pacing, and compositional organisation are not incidental aesthetic elements, but functional mechanisms for shaping temporal orientation and affective attunement. Entire perceptual and emotional trajectories can be modulated: '...achieving a tight control over viewers' brains during a movie requires, in most cases, intentional construction of the film's sequence through aesthetic means' (Hasson et al., 2008, p. 9). The principle extends beyond any single domain: structured environments synchronise what it feels like to perceive, attend, and care. This mechanism is further intensified through the auditory dimension. Sound does not merely accompany perception; it modulates the distribution of attention itself. When music is present, individuals exhibit increased attentional engagement relative to silent conditions, indexed by changes in brain activity associated with attention (see for example Kwon et al., 2022). What is crucial is not simply that attention increases, but that it is externally regulated. The auditory layer elevates arousal and stabilises focus, such that individuals '…pay more attention to the visual image of the footage when background music is available' (Kwon et al., 2022, p. 7). Attention becomes more tightly coupled to the structured flow of stimuli, reducing variability in perceptual engagement. Sound operates as an affective infrastructure that sustains alertness, synchronises cognitive rhythms, and channels perceptual energy. These dynamics extend beyond any isolated aesthetic setting into the texture of everyday environments. What emerges is not merely multimodal enhancement, but the pre-structuring of affective response. Emotional tone, semantic valence, and mnemonic trace become mediated in advance by contextual cues (Choen, 2010; Dasovich-Wilson et al., 2022). Repeated exposure to patterned cues—variations in tone, colour, sequence, or signal—can become reliable triggers, particularly when delivered at moments of susceptibility such as fatigue, boredom, or loneliness. What begins as synchronisation gradually approaches conditioned response: patterned stimuli eliciting patterned reactions, until response arrives with minimal deliberation—instinct no longer as embodied openness to the world, but as reflex tuned by environmental regularities. This is not a discussion confined to cinema or to media in any narrow sense. It concerns the structuring of perceptual environments as such. Wherever attention can be patterned, wherever salience can be ranked, wherever affect can be entrained, the same principle applies.

If this work has argued about anything, it is that the collapse of shared frameworks does not leave a vacuum. Something fills it. After the collapse of meaning, what awaits is not silence, but optimisation. Where metaphysical grounding recedes, algorithmic prediction advances. Where shared narratives weaken, ranking systems, recommendation engines, and anticipatory infrastructures begin to organise salience in their place. The future after collapse is not chaos. It is modulation. In the absence of stable symbolic anchors, prediction becomes the new orientation device. Behaviour is inferred before it is declared. Preference is anticipated before it is articulated. Relevance is calculated before it is judged. What was once negotiated collectively through narrative and tradition is increasingly managed procedurally through data.

The question, then, is not whether collapse occurred. It is what follows it. If orientation is no longer grounded in shared meaning, it will be guided by systems that pre-structure perception. If instinct is no longer cultivated through embodied encounter, it will be tuned by patterned environments. The danger is not annihilation of the subject, but its smooth integration into architectures that optimise response while narrowing deviation. And yet collapse does not eliminate responsibility. It intensifies it. The future after collapse will not be decided by whether technology advances. It will be decided by whether judgement can still emerge within conditions that continuously anticipate it. At stake is whether the subject becomes a predictable output of engineered environments—or remains capable of deviation. That is the question that remains.

Bibliography

Choen, A. J. (2010). Music as a source of emotion in film. In P. N. Juslin & J. A. Sloboda (Eds.), *Handbook of music and emotion: Theory, research, applications* (pp. 879–909). Oxford University Press.

Dasovich-Wilson, J. N., Thompson, M., & Saarikallio, S. (2022). Exploring music video experiences and their influence on music perception. *Music & Science, 5*, 20592043221117651. https://doi.org/10.1177/20592043221117651

Hasson, U., Landesman, O., Knappmeyer, B., Vallines, I., Rubin, N., & Heeger, D. J. (2008). Neurocinematics: The neuroscience of film. *Projections, 2*(1), 1–26. https://doi.org/10.3167/proj.2008.020102

Kwon, Y.-S., Lee, J., & Lee, S. (S.). (2022). The impact of background music on film audience's attentional processes: Electroencephalography alpha-rhythm and event-related potential analyses. *Frontiers in Psychology, 13*. https://doi.org/10.3389/fpsyg.2022.933497

Liu, Q., Lin, Y., & Zhang, W. (2025). Intersubject correlation as a predictor of attention: A systematic review. *BMC Psychology, 13*(1), 546. https://doi.org/10.1186/s40359-025-02879-7

MIX
Papier aus verantwortungsvollen Quellen
Paper from responsible sources
FSC® C105338

If you have any concerns about our products,
you can contact us on
ProductSafety@springernature.com

In case Publisher is established outside the EU,
the EU authorized representative is:
Springer Nature Customer Service Center GmbH
Europaplatz 3, 69115 Heidelberg, Germany

Printed by Libri Plureos GmbH
in Hamburg, Germany